S0-AAD-964

Natascha Kampusch
10 Years of Freedom

# Natascha Kampusch
with Heike Gronemeier

# *10 Years of Freedom*

Translated by Jill Kreuer

**Dachbuch**
Verlag

Dachbuch Verlag

Published by Dachbuch Verlag GmbH, Vienna

ISBN 978-3-9504426-0-1

*10 Jahre Freiheit* first published in Germany by Ullstein Buchverlage 2016
First published in English by Dachbuch Verlag 2017

Copyright © 2017 Ullstein Buchverlage GmbH, Berlin
Translation © 2017 Jill Kreuer
All rights reserverd

Typeset by Dachbuch Verlag GmbH, Vienna
Cover design by Dachbuch Verlag GmbH, Vienna
Cover photo by Kristof Gyselinck
Printed and bounded by Ingram Book Group LLC, La Vergne
Printed in Great Britain, USA, Canada, Australia

Dedicated to all the courageous women who are fighting for their independence in the hopes of being free to live the life that they choose. Dedicated to all those who have succeeded in finding a resolution to a seemingly hopeless situation.

I also dedicate this book to all those forced to experience terrible violence and abuse in childhood without ever receiving outside help. I hope that one day they will be able to overcome their pain and rediscover their true selves. Do not give up, no matter how long the journey before you may appear to be. The last ten years have shown me above all that freedom first takes root in the soul, slowly making its way from deep inside to reach the outside world.

# Contents

# *Prologue*

Believe in yourself – you are of value. Find comfort – it
will be okay. Be strong.
Persevere – you will make it. You will be rewarded.
Courage. There is always hope.
Never give up! Trust yourself!! Trust in the future. Ev-
erything will be okay. Good luck!
If you set a goal for yourself and work toward it, you
will <u>reach</u> your objective. Nothing can kill you. Be
brave. Everything others do to you should not be your
problem. Free yourself.
Hard work pays off. In the end you <u>always</u> get what <u>you</u>
<u>want</u>. What doesn't kill you makes you stronger.
The path to your goal may be difficult, but it will be
easier with every step you take!
You can take everything they dish out if you must.
Whenever he rips you to shreds, or is cruel and indiffer-
ent, it is not your problem. It is his!

I wrote all of these lines (including all of the spelling and punctuation
mistakes in the original German) during my captivity using a number
of different coloured pencils on the back of a wall calendar. Additionally, I even circled a number of phrases that I thought were particularly

important. My handwriting was a bit awkward. There was not a lot of room on the page, resulting in one sentence, one line flowing seamlessly into the next. Just like everything in that tiny room flowed together. Days and nights, minutes and hours, light and darkness. Dreams and reality, tense wakefulness and restless sleep. A life, shrunk down to just a few square metres, surrounded by thick, massive walls. Untraceable, perhaps long forgotten and abandoned, as my kidnapper constantly tried to convince me.

When I wrote these lines, I was 10 or 11 years old. I don't remember exactly. I was convinced that these lines, these phrases that gave me courage would only be of importance down here in my underground dungeon. That they would help me through the many years of my captivity, however long that would be. That they would help me find separation between myself and my kidnapper and his actions, no matter what he did to me. Back then I most certainly never thought that these words would be of importance to me once my captivity was ended.

The massive walls of my dungeon, over a half-metre thick and made from gravel, concrete and metal, would be replaced by other walls after my escape. At first glance, these are much more transparent, seemingly easier to penetrate. But even today I have been unable to fully overcome them. Also because new walls are continually being added. Like fortification rings limiting my newfound freedom again and again, the freedom I had placed so much hope in, that I had envisioned as being so infinitely good and wonderful during my captivity. These are limits that I could run at as much as I liked, and they never gave an inch. Limits that seem so arbitrary, thereby depriving me of resources for overcoming them. Running at these walls has always been a setback to my growth, to my attempt to reconcile myself with life, my life.

Many of these rings originated from the outside, arising from the public's interest in me, which at some point knew no bounds. There was a great deal of empathy and honest compassion, but also a lack of tact and sensitivity to ethics and morals, as well as to my needs as a victim, even though I had never wanted to see myself that way. In the beginning messages of sympathy were mixed in with the demands and expectations, and facts that were actually quite clear gave way to speculation and crude theories. Many of those who investigated the crime or became involved after my escape failed to consider the people they affected, seeing only an opportunity to become famous, if only for the fleeting minutes of a single interview.

As far as that is concerned, the kidnapping resulted in numerous victims, both direct and indirect. This includes my parents and my family. I know that they went through hell many times over in the eight and a half years of my captivity, torn apart by self-recrimination and the inability to bring about any change in their situation. Accused and condemned, eyed mistrustfully, wavering between hope and resignation, and the willing prey of the media looking to nab the "ultimate inside story". My classmates, who in their shock turned the blame on themselves and lived in fear of experiencing a fate similar to mine. The many investigators and emergency crews, the pressure of having to produce results despite very few leads. The fear of failure, actual mistakes, a stream of new theories about my disappearance or my time in captivity. All of this was a mixture that has left a very bitter taste in its wake even today.

I myself have become a public person. Not because that is something that I have always wanted, but rather because the "Kampusch case" has never found a peaceful conclusion. Conspiracy theorists, journalists, actual or self-proclaimed investigators, politicians and members of the judicial system – everybody is pursuing their own agenda, abusing me for purposes I have no control over, and whose underlying motives have often not become apparent until after the fact. Getting to the bottom of the case and acting in the interest of the victim were sometimes just a smokescreen.

I have been accused of having planned the kidnapping myself, of covering for possible accomplices, of lying, of wallowing in self-pity and of constantly making a profit off of a story that never could have happened the way I have repeatedly said it did. After all, a victim, who had undergone years of martyrdom, would never look like me.

I had had enough time to prepare myself for Day X, even if everything has actually turned out quite differently and the full force of it has completely overwhelmed me. I did not wait for a rescuer from the outside to save me, or hope for a miracle, but I rescued myself when I was ready to do so in my mind and when an opportunity arose. I maintained control and did not give myself over to my fate. During the eight and half years of my captivity I played the role that the kidnapper had reserved for me only in part. But I never accepted it as my role in life. I never gave up my inner identity, never allowed my will to be broken. If that had happened, I would probably not have survived all those years.

The strength that allowed me to adapt to such a surreal situation was then held up as a character defect after my escape. As alleged evidence that it couldn't have been as bad as all that. Instead of being happy for me that I had emerged from those long years more or less in one piece, the idea now was to tear me down. The enthusiasm about the "Miracle of Strasshof" was transformed into envy, resentment and in some cases an unabashed hate that lashed out at me primarily from the protective anonymity of the Internet. This is a form of hate that I still fail to fully comprehend today.

It even went so far as to force me to justify myself for a crime that was perpetrated against me. Because the kidnapper was no longer at hand, there was no "Priklopil case". Just the "Kampusch case". In a way, I was made to pay for the uncertainty that the abduction unleashed in society. A criminal act perpetrated by a single man revealed how thin the veneer of civilization is that coats the surface of our society. We are the good guys. Evil lurks in the depths. It must wear an evil grimace. It must be obvious. And yet, it is not. In the end, that is nothing more than an enormous self-deception. When criminals like Josef Fritzl are labelled "monster" or "beast", thereby excluding them from the norm and consigning them to a "superhumanly cruel" dimension, we perhaps hope to receive a kind of absolution. We couldn't have anticipated such a thing. After all, that goes beyond even our imaginative capacities, we say to ourselves. That is certainly correct. But is it not also the case that "society" – and here it is not my intention to overgeneralize – continually averts its eyes, ducks its head and allows events to take their course, because it cannot come to grips with the fact that evil lives among us, in our neighbourhoods and in our families?

It is precisely this that leads to an enormous feeling of insecurity. This is precisely what we cannot cope with, tempting us at least to mistakenly conjure up an enormous conspiracy pulling the strings. The act of an individual man, who in actuality was actually quite nice, middle-class, with a properly mowed lawn, perhaps a "mama's boy", but always friendly – that cannot be, and must not be allowed to stand. It must be even more monstrous, and we must read even more into it, so that we can cope with the thought of it.

I was forced to cope with both. The captivity and the vicarious "indictment" afterward. At times it seemed to me like children trying to rescue a strange bug. In fighting over who got to hold it, they ended up squashing it in their zeal. I was forced to conform to so many images, play so many roles that were imposed on me all at once that I sometimes wondered who I actually was. Most people developed their own image of me as a person. Nothing is as alienating as being confronted with yourself. This kind of self-examination is difficult within the confines of your own four walls, but it is much, much more difficult when it takes place in the public eye. Subjectively. every single journalist, everyone on the street had a much better understanding of myself and the story of my life than I did myself. About what I thought, what I needed, what I felt, how I was to act. Sometimes I felt as if I would never be able to live up to Natascha Kampusch. I was not part icon, part saint, something akin to the Virgin Mary that some cast me as on the basis of a photograph that was published alongside my first interviews. I was not an alien or an angel who had been sent to found a new Church of the Enlightened.

I was not a carbon copy of people who had lived through trauma themselves and hoped I could offer them a solution to their situation. And I was not the slut, the piece of filth that had to be ground just a bit deeper into the mud for it to finally understand what it really meant to eat dirt. And not a template for crude fantasies about the correct way to treat girls and women, not an object for further humiliation and debasement. God knows I had experienced that long enough.

I had fled one enemy, and all at once I had gained hundreds more, and in some Internet chat rooms even thousands. Without me having known any one of them or having had any kind of connection to any of them personally. Mainly, however, I was not prepared to be exposed to the "outside world" so defencelessly. After all, this "outside world" had so many facets that I couldn't have been prepared for. In my underground dungeon I had learned at some point what behaviour would elicit which reaction and/or punishment. In a way, the kidnapper was in fact very transparent. He knew what buttons he had to push to wound me, and after several years I knew what his buttons were as well.

Cut the power, turn off the lights, take away the batteries for the Walkman, deprive me of food. Beatings and other kinds of mistreatment. My refusal to call him "Lord". The power to do a slipshod cleaning job and leave behind a hair or fingerprints that could prove his undoing. The constant fear, mainly later, when I stood with him in the checkout line at the "Billa" supermarket or at the DIY chain that we would be discovered and people would notice me. There were very few strings that I held in my hand during my captivity, and it took me quite a long time until I realized that I held those strings and that I could sometimes manipulate them.

Outside, in the world of the good people, I hardly stood a chance. It was no longer a matter of predefined reactions, of an action, a transgression and punishment or reward. It was a matter of manifold interests, of much more subtle forms of punishment and reward. It was extremely trying for me that the "Kampusch case" continued to smoulder, although the case should have been closed long ago with the solving of the actual crime. The increasingly hair-raising rumours meant that I could find no peace. At the beginning I was outraged. Then angry. Then only sad. I tortured myself by asking what it was about me that made people reject me and brand me as someone that in a way was capable of deeds even more evil than the kidnapper himself had committed. The worst accusation that could be levelled at me was barely insulting enough for them. I did not understand why the boundaries had come to be so blurred. Perhaps because I unwittingly held a mirror up to some people or parts of society. And looking into that mirror frightened them. Frightened them of the depths, of repression, but also of allowing strengths and weaknesses to show.

I really believed that my escape would mark the beginning of what I referred to once in an interview as my "third life". A completely new phase, a new beginning, full of energy and opportunities. I underestimated how much and for how long external forces would compel me to allow my dark past to take up space in my life again and again. There were phases where I was actually convinced that I could brush off my past, removing it from me much like a glove. Without being confronted with memories of my prior existence in confinement. As if my memory had been erased and I would now lead a completely new life.

That figurative glove was one that over time took on the meaning of a gauntlet. I myself know well enough that I did not lose my memory, and that glove, with its dark fingers, will always serve to remind me that I have a past that I did not seek out myself, but will carry with me all my life. I know this, and I am prepared to deal with it. And I will deal with it somehow, at times rather well, at other times not so well. The fact that others would throw down their very own gauntlets in front of me was something I had not anticipated. And their motives are sometimes even more painful to me than some of the abuse I experienced from my kidnapper. That abuse was at least out in the open.

I completely underestimated how much strength it would cost me to attempt closure for something where closure apparently cannot or must not be achieved. Every time I think that I can do it, that I'm headed in the right direction, "the world" shows me how wrong I am. Sometimes it is my inner world, my memories that prevent me from severing my ties to the past. Often enough it is my external world that appears to have an interest in preventing me from living my life. As if consigning me to a cell much like the one I had been locked up in as a matter of reality for many long years. But this is one I am apparently not allowed to escape.

Because just as the kidnapper had to be made larger than life so that his crime could be bearable, the victim too must be assigned a role. Either to be broken for the rest of his or her life or to deal with the pressure of expectations that can never be lived up to. I don't know whether somebody on the outside looking in would say that I was a failure. For example, because I completed my compulsory secondary education, but not yet my professional training. I don't know whether I will be considered a failure in the future. It always depends on the benchmarks used to determine "failure". For me it is a triumph simply that I am still alive. That I am capable of withstanding everything that has been thrown at me from the outside, also and especially in the last ten years. The fact that I can, for the most part, live independently and self-sufficiently.

I navigate my life between the two extremes of strength as a survivor and weakness as a victim. Maybe recognizing this fact requires taking a second look. What people often interpret as arrogance or haughtiness on my part was in many cases nothing more than retreat, a sign of insecurity. A protective armour that I built up slowly over the years from my childhood and was forced to finish constructing in my captivity. I underestimated how important it would still be once I had gained my freedom. Words can be very hurtful. Certain mechanisms in society can cause painful wounds as well. In some cases I was forced in a very bitter way to recognize interconnections that many were blind to their entire lives, never having had to take notice of them. There are days where I wish that I could have been spared exactly this. And while I write these lines, I know that these are statements that many will interpret as pure self-pity. They will elicit comments on blogs, such as "Why don't you go back in the cellar then". When they find out that I've written another book, many will say, "You don't always have to go on making yourself all important. Nobody can stand to look at your mug in the media anymore anyway."

I'm ready for it. And yet, I still don't want to give up my belief in the good in people. Nor in my courage, if that's what you want to call it, to address issues I think are important.

In an interview three years after my escape, I once said that I felt like an uprooted orchid, a plant that is washed up somewhere, lays down roots for short time, and then is forced to move on. It is planted where other people would like to have it and see it. I hope that this book will help generate some understanding for my need to grow and to thrive where and how I would like. And that it helps to foster reconciliation by providing a second look, a look behind the façade. And I would like to achieve closure to a story, in which at some point everyone has been at the mercy of outside forces.

I would like to continue to trust in myself and the future. I only have one life to live, and I would like to take full advantage of it. Even if my path in life, toward my future may be difficult, it is getting easier with every step I take. Every day in freedom is a gift that I try to receive with happiness and gratitude. But also with courage and the energy to move forward.

Nelson Mandela once said that being free not only means removing your own fetters, but living a life that also respects and fosters the freedom of others. I must remove my fetters myself – just like anyone else …

# Caught between "Kaspar Hauser" and "Global Sensation"

## *The first few weeks of my new life*

> Like a swarm of bees everybody was buzzing around
> me. Everyone thought that there was something to be
> plumbed from her and her story. Figuratively speaking,
> I came crawling out of a hole, and the first thing that
> I saw were contracts. Everybody said, you only have to
> sign here, you only have to do what we tell you, and
> everything will be okay.

The first few days of my new life in freedom were characterized, if you will, by a lack of freedom. It was actually meant to be a protected, gentle return to the world, as shielded as possible from the media storm raging outside, which broke out with an unanticipated intensity upon my escape and after reports that Natascha Kampusch, who had been missing for years, had surfaced once again. The choice for my first new home for the time being fell on the Vienna General Hospital (AKH), particularly as I needed to be given a thorough medical examination after eight and a half years in an underground dungeon. After all, my time in captivity had also left behind clear physical scars.

I had serious problems with my eyes and was extremely sensitive to changes between light and dark. It was difficult for me to focus on one point, as my eyes continued to wander restlessly back and forth. When I felt overwhelmed – and in my first few days actually everything felt over-whelming – I began to roll my eyes around, which must have seemed like a tick to observers. A quirk from my time in the cellar.

I had problems with balance and motor skills, and had difficulty judging distances. Walking across a larger room all by myself was a chal-lenge. I needed something or someone I could hold on to so that I could put one foot in front of the other with confidence. The restrictions on my scope of movement, as dictated by the walls that had surrounded me for years, were burned into my brain. Those walls were an instrument of torture and torment on one hand, but had also provided me with safety and protection on the other. When I was allowed to leave them for the first time, the size of the house sitting on top of the underground dun-geon terrified me.

I was even afraid of the stairs leading up to the ground level, which according to the kidnapper were lined with numerous explosive traps that one false move could trigger at any time. In my underground room I was able over time to prepare myself for when the kidnapper came. I could hear the scraping noise of him pushing the safe aside, and I could estimate how long it would take for him to crawl through the small en-trance way and operate the mechanism for the heavy door. Upstairs in the house, when I was forced to work for him, I felt more unprotected, much more directly exposed to his arbitrary behaviour and mood swings.

Malnourishment meant that I had developed a number of allergies, and my skin and my stomach reacted sensitively to any change. The first images after my escape broadcast on television and published in the print media showed the hem of my colourful summer dress beneath the blue blanket, and underneath my thin legs. My chalk white skin was covered with red marks, brownish spots and bruises.

All my years in captivity I had never once seen a doctor. Wounds inflicted on me by the kidnapper, such as burns caused by boiling water on my hands and arms, had never been professionally treated. Looking back I was certainly lucky that I never contracted a serious infection. After all the split personality of the kidnapper, so contemptuous of other human beings, was also evident in how he dealt with the issue of my health.

On the one hand, he was nearly hysterical when it came to maintaining a supposedly healthy diet. Food seemed to him to be fundamentally suspicious. Large food companies were all in league with one another, trying to systematically and slowly poison humanity with contaminated foodstuffs. Spices primarily were full of radiation and had to be avoided under all circumstances. Later it was carbohydrates, sugar and even fruit that he banned from our menu – due to the poisons in the fruit peels. At the same time he had no problem in starving me for days on end if I was "too rebellious". The stomach cramps and dizziness I suffered from were a just punishment for my transgressions. Even today I still have a problematic relationship with food.

I can still remember that a program was recorded in December 2006 showing my "first Christmas in freedom". After a half hour I called one of my lawyers on the phone, saying, "I'm in Gänserndorf.* Please come immediately. Everything is so complicated." The house being used for the filming belonged to an employee of the Austrian Broadcasting System (ORF). Out in front of the house was a large truck with furniture that people were using to redecorate the house. Everybody was bustling about, cables were everywhere, and I was sitting alone on the couch, like something somebody had ordered and forgotten to pick up. Nobody took the time to see how alone I was in the middle of all those people.

---

* A town in Lower Austria, north-east of Vienna.

20

A bit later, a catering company delivered boxes with rolls and sandwiches. People grabbed the food as they were walking by. They ate while walking or standing; crumbs spilled onto the carpets, and tomato and mayonnaise landed on the floor. I could only sit there in shock at how little respect people were showing for the food. Even a half year after escaping, the mechanisms of my underground dungeon were still in perfect working order. Food had to be earned. "Don't wolf it down, otherwise there won't be any more. Now you've made a mess of yourself again." Once while I was removing a piece of fish from the pan, a piece of breading had fallen off. The kidnapper grabbed my helping and poured dishwashing liquid over it so that I would learn not to make such a mess.

Of paramount importance above all else: cleanliness. Germs were the worst evil. They lurked everywhere, dangerously invisible vectors of disease. Priklopil was genuinely compulsive about cleaning in a way that certainly did not only stem from his desire to remove every minuscule trace of me. A hair from my head, a piece of dead skin, fingerprint, nothing could be left behind in the house to be discovered. Aside from the paranoia that he increasingly gave into over the years, he was also terrified of diseases that could be triggered by germs, viruses or bacteria.

At the same time he had no problem with inflicting the most severe punches and kicks on me, including bloody injuries. Once I slipped on the stairs going down into my underground dungeon and hit my head on the steps, knocking me unconscious for a moment. When I came to again, I was severely nauseous; there was nothing but a hammering in my head that wouldn't stop. I was afraid that I could have fractured my skull. Over the next several days I could only lie in bed motionless. As soon as I lifted my head, my vision would go black. All of that was of no interest to the kidnapper. Quite the opposite, he punished me for my "stupid behaviour" because I had dropped a glass bowl when I fell and the steps had been dirtied by my blood. That was the moment it finally became fully clear to me that he would prefer to let me die than to get help, even in an acute emergency.

I had to learn to tolerate and live with pain. I had to learn to tolerate hunger and to live with that torturous feeling that numbs all of your senses, makes you dizzy and even makes you lose your grip on reality. After an extended starvation phase, I could only take in food by the spoonful. The smell, the texture, everything that I had fantasized about in the days before was now too much. Swallowing felt like downright choking, and afterwards my stomach burned like fire, and my entire abdomen was swollen.

\*

After my escape the marks of my years of captivity were clearly visible on the outside. But nobody knew whether or not I had suffered organ damage. The doctors at the Vienna General Hospital were to shed light on all of that, and my mental well-being as well.

I could not be admitted to a normal freely-accessible floor for security reasons. So the decision was made to place me on the paediatric psychiatry floor. Because I was already legally an adult, I had to "admit" myself so that I could remain in the hospital by law.

I was admitted to the locked ward, which meant that patients who posed a danger to themselves or others were unable to open the doors to their rooms from the inside. With just a few minor adjustments, the door handle can be removed if needed. Additionally, security guards were posted to the ward and guarded the entrance to my room today and night. Just as nobody could come in, I was not allowed to go out either in the beginning.

On one hand, this was a good idea, because I was able to collect myself in this protected space and refocus my mental resources. But on the other hand, it was completely absurd. I had just regained my freedom, and again I was locked away. And what I had longed for most of all toward the end of my captivity was something I could not have during this initial phase: I wanted autonomy; I wanted to decide for myself. The kidnapper, who had styled himself the "lord and master" over my life, was now in a way replaced by an entire team that now monitored and dictated every one of my steps.

Here I would like to ensure that there is no misunderstanding. When I make this comparison, it is of course not about the methods and the underlying motives, which could not have been more different. The point of comparison was what the situation triggered in me emotionally. In a way, I was once again reduced to object status even though that was probably not fully apparent to the people who were charged with my care. The focus was only on my protection, my mental and physical health and stability.

Shortly after my escape a guardianship commission was established to look after my well-being, initially made up of: Prof. Dr. Ernst Berger from the Rosenhügel Neurological Rehabilitation Centre, at the time a consultant to the Psychosocial Services of the City of Vienna and in that capacity "Municipal Project Head" for paediatric psychiatric care; Prof. Dr. Max Friedrich, head of the University Hospital for Paediatric Neuropsychiatry; Monika Pinterits, Ombudsperson for Children and Young People of the City of Vienna, and Udo Jesionek, the head of the victims' assistance organization "Weißer Ring".

That was the only decision that I made for myself while I was still at the police station I had been brought to just after my escape. I knew of the organization from the radio; once down in my dungeon I had heard a broadcast on victims of violent crimes. I thought at the time that they would be right for me. At the police station I also met Prof. Dr. Ernst Berger for the first time, who carried out an initial psychological examination of me after my first questioning by police and explained the next steps to me. He was also the one who suggested a temporary stay in the hospital and told me about his friend Max, considered a genius in his field.

Added to the mix was a media consultant and an attorney from the Vienna Children and Youth Ombudsperson's Office, who was introduced to me at the hospital. He had a very pleasant and reserved way about him, and our conversation went actually pretty well, as I saw it. I was relieved that an experienced victims' attorney was to take my case. Unfortunately, he withdrew from the case after only four days, saying that he could not manage it all on his own. He told me to look for a large law firm that was experienced in handling such complex cases, particularly one that generated such intense public interest.

Suddenly one of the pillars of my team had broken away. The next was to follow in September. The media consultant who had been provided to me was faced with the enormous task of dealing with the many requests from Austrian and foreign print and broadcast media. We needed to ensure that the reporting was as serious as possible, controlling the flow of information with the main focus on protecting me. Also at stake was an enormous profit-making enterprise, he said.

When it became clear that the public pressure would not subside and that I had to make some kind of statement, we drew up a press strategy, providing for a television interview and two interviews with the print media. After I had gotten through all of that more or less in one piece, my media consultant brought an armful of flowers with him to the hospital. A nice gesture for the nurses and for myself. He was beaming from ear to ear when he came into my room and sat down on one of the chairs.

What came next completely stunned me. He just came right out with it, not mincing any words. I was completely taken aback. In the first few days and weeks there was absolutely nobody who showed me more devastatingly clearly that the preservation of my interests in terms and protecting me as a victim was not going to be standard operating procedure. My unusual case involved diverse interests of a wide variety of people involved. I was the object that made all of it possible. The object of analysis, of ambition, of her own fame, the "golden goose" that had to

24

be plucked as soon as possible. After all, according to a representative of the press at the time, the story was going to be considered journalistically dead in four weeks and out of the media spotlight.

The world of good people had hit a clear snag. This kind of focus on selfish interests disturbed me. I can understand that people were in over their heads with the case, or even with me. Everybody was in completely uncharted territory, and nobody was prepared for it. But my experience very early on, sadly, was that I was being moved around on a chessboard depending on which move, or whose interests my position benefitted most. A board game whose rules I did not, or could not know. In my dungeon the rules and the roles were clearly defined. I was only a pawn until I slowly redefined my assigned role. Until I had determined what was possible, until I asserted my position, with all of the humiliations and punishments that resulted.

Here I was no longer a pawn in the sick world of the kidnapper's mind, caught up in his fantasies, but rather surrounded by people who are supposed to advocate on my behalf. Most of them certainly did, but at least a few of them made me feel that I was being instrumentalized in a completely different way. Although they were all experienced and respected experts in their fields, I was also a bit like a global sensation for them after all. My story eclipsed everything that had come before, promising to attract attention from far beyond Austria's borders. Nobody had any kind of blueprint for how to deal with anyone like me "correctly", but everybody had an interest in this "case". Unfortunately their interests were not always entirely altruistic.

*

After I had undergone all of the normal medical examinations, I was made to take various intelligence tests, and my brain was scanned on several occasions. As if the doctors were looking for that one particular trait, that one particular difference that could provide the answer to why I had survived my time in captivity relatively unscathed, at least at first glance. They were likely hoping to produce images spit out by all manner of medical equipment pointing to an area of the brain with a label reading "location of the centre for Natascha Kampusch's special resilience capabilities." The images were completely normal, with no anomalies of any kind.

Just a few days after my escape one of the doctors put a piece of paper in front of me to sign. I was to agree to be available for the next ten years exclusively for study purposes. Like a rare animal, put on display the world over and taken from lecture hall to lecture hall, while its behaviour, its physical and mental condition were analyzed and evaluated by the attending experts in front of a crowd of students.

From the point of view of the doctors, psychiatrists and psychologists I may in fact have been an interesting object of study. However, those interests did not intersect very much with the idea of protecting me – and that is exactly why the meeting of advisors and advocates had actually been called, and exactly why I had temporarily admitted myself to the Vienna General Hospital. I will never forget the time that everybody was sitting in my room, including the two new attorneys who had taken my case in the meantime. The discussion about what was to happen next became so heated that it would not have taken much for the gentleman to come to blows. Everybody was pulling me in a different direction, as if they wanted to tear me apart.

The patients on the psychiatric floor were the most normal aspect in all of this insanity. Most of them were younger than I was, suffered from eating disorders such as anorexia or bulimia, or engaged in cutting in order to dull their inner pain by injuring themselves on the outside. I participated in a number of group therapy sessions and was simply accepted by the other young people as somebody who also had their burden to bear, just like they did. Nobody asked how that burden had come about. Nobody was interested in performing an autopsy on it and conducting an evaluation. I was able to just sit with them, to talk about this and that and to enjoy a moment of peace.

I remember a 16-year-old boy in particular, who I met while waiting for an examination. He was in urgent need of an organ donation. His time was running out, and he knew that the worst case scenario meant that he would die soon. Even though I knew him for only a short time, our encounter meant something special to me. It showed me that in the end it is not that important how much time you spend with someone, but the fact that you had spent time with them at all. He was a person who had so much empathy, such an enormous will to live. He was extremely open and interested in other people. He was somebody who, despite experiencing extreme pain and the powerful effects of medication such as morphine, tried to live in the moment and to avoid giving negative emotions too much space. I don't know if it is possible to understand what I'm saying, but in a way the extreme degree of his fate made him a mirror for me. We did not have to talk; we could sit there and just be, while the rest of the time I felt like I was caught up in the swirling eddy of my new life. Everything was just spinning around me, and it was hard to catch my breath or even think. Sometimes I wished I were a cat and could just sit in a chair, staring into space, collecting myself, gathering energy. But there was no peace to be had.

I was overwhelmed by everything: the harsh, artificial lighting, the many noises, the smells, all of the meals to be eaten, all of the people. Everybody talked at the same time, and everybody wanted something: a conversation here, an examination there. A nurse was assigned to me, to accompany me to my examinations through the long corridors of the hospital, which I found frightening. Punctuating my day were questions asked again and again by the police, about my kidnapping, about the kidnapper and about my captivity, for hours on end.

The first details were leaked to the public very early on. And this time it again did not take very long for word to spread about where I was staying. A pseudonym had been arranged for people to address me when I was on the floor. A number of nurses, however, did not use it; one of them even levelled the charge at me that I probably thought I was someone special, but that I most certainly wasn't and that I should get used to living in the real world, and fast.

At times I felt like all I wanted was to shrink from that reality, as much as it offended me with its relentlessness, fluctuating between swallowing me up and spitting me out. I tried to make myself a small as possible, to let everything wash over me, and I promised myself that I would emancipate myself as quickly as possible from these decisions being imposed on me from the outside.

It was not a capricious idea on my part to give me a cover name. It was purely a security measure. If I had had my way, I would've much rather preferred to keep my own name. I was so happy to have it back again, even though I never particularly liked "Natascha" in the first place. I made the very conscious decision not to take on a new identity in conjunction with any kind of witness protection program. Or to go into hiding or emigrate. A new identity and a new background story would have had an impact on my entire environment. I wanted to resume the life I had once had, to pick up where I left off, no longer disassociating from any part of it. While I was in captivity disassociation and suppression were part of my everyday life. I was even forced to give up my name. A year after I was taken my kidnapper told me his idea, "You are no longer Natascha. You now belong to me. You are my creation." I wasn't anything anymore; all connection to my past, to my first life was to be completely eradicated. For months he had hammered into my brain that nobody was going to come looking for me anyway. Nobody missed me. My parents were happy to finally be rid of me. Otherwise they would have paid the ransom. Otherwise the police would have found me long ago. In order to completely sever ties, something my family had done long ago, I had to give up my name as the most visible token of my identity. He proposed "Maria", because both of his grandmothers had been

28

called Maria. When I naïvely told him that that was okay by me, and that I would quite like that because that was my middle name, one that I had always preferred to Natascha, Maria was no longer an option. He told me that I was a dumb cow, that I did not understand what the point was. "You no longer have a family. I am your family. I am your father, your mother, your grandma and your sisters. I am now your everything. You no longer have a past," he said. He hit me across the head and hissed that it couldn't possibly be that hard to find a new name.

My gaze fell on a calendar on the small desk in my underground dungeon. It contained a list of saints' days. I thumbed hurriedly through the pages, constantly waiting for the next blow to fall. Natascha, "strong, or born at Christmas", was in the calendar for December 1. Bibiana was in the calendar on December 2. For the next seven years of my captivity I was Bibiana, or "Bibi". However, on the inside I never gave up my identity this way, the way the kidnapper expected and demanded of me.

Once free I most definitely did not want to give it up. What happened to me could not simply be put in a drawer and given a new label. The second phase of my life was also a part of me, and I had to learn how to cope with it. I had to have the right to talk about it when I felt like it, and not to talk about it when I felt like it. As "Ms. Meier from Linz" I probably could have spared myself many a headache, but I could not have led my life. Instead I would've had to take on yet another role. As if I had fallen into a strange makeup pot and a costume box that would disguise me until I was unrecognizable.

I don't remember what cover name and what brief back-story they made up in the hospital. But the fact that not everybody stuck to it and the fact that even the "closed" floor was really an "open" one in many areas meant that word first travelled to the entire hospital about who was a "patient" there. When I took a few steps out onto the corridor, I sometimes felt like I was in a zoo. Other patients or visitors would be standing in front of the doors to the floor, all eager to get a look at me. I felt like I was enclosed behind safety glass; you can look, but don't feed the animals.

And it wasn't far from the hospital grapevine to the outside world. Photographers climbed trees waiting to take the first picture of me. Reporters tried to sneak into the hospital disguised as nurses. A newspaper wrote that I had the "most sought-after face in the world." Because nobody had seen it, but everybody wanted to know what the "cellar girl" looked like.

The media frenzy had already begun on the day of my escape. A number of journalists had apparently been listening to the police radio, when it was reported on 23 August 2006 that possibly a "confused young woman" had appeared in an n garden, claiming to have been kidnapped years ago. The police headquarters in the Lower Austrian capital of St. Pölten, which received the emergency call around 2 PM, sent a police car from Gänserndorf to Strasshof to verify her, my identity.

Just a few hours later my mother got a call from a journalist who had interviewed her from time to time over the years. It was clear that she would not call simply out of the blue to have a chat, but only if there was something she wanted or if there was a new development in the case. After beating around the bush a while – she did not want to raise any false hopes – the reporter finally divulged that her missing daughter Natascha may have been taken to the police station in Deutsch-Wagram. It took a while after that call for the criminal police office to phone my mother to tell her that it was "99 percent certain" that her long years of waiting and hoping were over.

In August 2006 my mother had gone to Annaberg, near the pilgrimage site of Mariazell in Lower Austria, with my half-sister Sabina and my nieces and nephews for a few days of holiday. The farm where they were staying had become almost like a second home for her and the children over the last several years. Every year she lit a candle for me in the basilica. That year she did not. On that day in August the chapel was closed for renovations. A strange coincidence.

When she came out of the farmhouse, it wasn't just the grey police Volkswagen waiting to bring her to me, but camera teams and reporters from the regional broadcaster of the Austrian broadcasting system were on hand as well, peppering her with questions that she could not answer. And after they had taken down my personal information at the police station in Deutsch-Wagram and I was taken to an anteroom for questioning by police officers, members of the gutter press took up their positions outside.

For months in captivity I had imagined what my escape might be like and how life would go on afterwards. However, the police had no pre-conceived strategy they could have pulled out of a drawer somewhere. Looking back, the mood was very strange, a mixture of joy, incredulousness and remarkable naïveté. I still remember that I asked them several times to protect me.

On one hand from the kidnapper, as at that time nobody knew anything about what had happened to him. I was afraid that he would end up nabbing me again, that he would make good on his threats to kill everybody, should I ever dare to flee. I was afraid that he would hurt my parents or even an innocent bystander in his fury or desperation. And I was afraid that he would make good on his threat to kill himself. Escape meant death. For me, for everybody I encountered along the way, for him. Over the last several years it had been a kind of tacit agreement between the two of us, that only one of us would survive if I should run away. If I had really managed to do it, if here at the station I had eluded his grasp, sooner or later I would be responsible for a person's death.

I know the statements I have made in the past on that count have not always been understood. But I was simply of the opinion that you have to assume responsibility for your actions. And my actions put the kidnapper in a position from which there was no escape for him, which only pointed in one direction. Once I even did the math for him, telling him that he would be 60 when he got out of prison, if he were to let me go free and turn himself in to the police. However, the forcible confinement of a person for longer than a month is punishable by a maximum of 10 years in prison in Austria, and not by 20, as I had thought. At the time he said that he would not survive his sentence in prison, with all the dirt, germs and the other prisoners. They were certain to be violent and brutal, he thought. To my ears it seemed like cruel irony. But in his own twisted perception of himself and the world, it was only logical.

Aside from the kidnapper, I also wanted to be protected somewhat from the world outside. Not from freedom, but from what was wrapped up in this newfound freedom. During my initial time in captivity I was completely cut off from the outside world. I existed within a closed system. Or perhaps I should say in two closed systems. In the world of the kidnapper and in the world of my imagination. The rest of the world entered into my isolation only after a time by way of books or cassette tapes with audio plays for children; later on I was allowed to listen to selected frequencies on a radio and watch certain TV channels or programs recorded by the kidnapper. In this way the media gradually became my window to the world. And it was the media that enabled me to measure the passage of time day after day in my underground dungeon.

Much, much later, when he was certain that he had moulded "his creature" sufficiently, I was also allowed to watch "trash TV" from time to time. For Priklopil this tripe, broadcast primarily on private commercial TV channels, was a window into the degenerate world of the underclass, where people are unemployed, drunk, violent and tacky. Totally different from his perfect family, whose obvious problems were hidden behind a whitewashed façade and couldn't easily be seen. However, for years many people attributed exactly these characteristics to my family. No wonder that the girl "ran away", growing up in such an environment, they said. These insults reached a low point in the statements made by a former justice of the Austrian Supreme Court*, who said that I could have been inclined to accept the offer of an "alternative life far from my

---

* In this instance it was the former president of the Austrian Supreme Court (OGH); "Irritie-

32

family and temptingly portrayed" by the kidnapper.

I would've liked to trade places with these people, sitting behind their large desks, in their large, posh flats, pontificating on about the so-called precariat, that it is obviously so terrible that a person would willingly lock themselves in a tiny hole just to get away from it all. Families that did not fit the proper mould could simply not produce anything good, they opined. Victims that did not fit the proper mould, like I was and still am, can only have put themselves in such a situation voluntarily, not by force. By either having planned the kidnapping themselves or, once kidnapped, by accepting this life joyfully as an alternative, they stated.

I sometimes wonder what boxes people who make such nonsensical statements think in. What perception do they have of the world and the people in it, and thereby of themselves? It must be one full of hate, contempt and devoid of any shred of empathy and at the same time completely out of touch with reality.

*

Inspired by the success of the commercial broadcasters, the public broadcasters quickly followed suit with tabloid magazine shows aimed at satisfying the audience's appetite for the sensational. These shows, which were my window to the world, taught me a great deal about these mechanisms, the unearthing of supposed secrets and scandals, the hyping of triviality into enormous sensationalism.

The end to my kidnapping case was now an actual sensation that did not need any further hyping whatsoever. Just the fact that I had survived at all was an achievement, and for such an incredibly long period of time.

---

rende Aussagen von Ex-OGH-Präsident", see: wiev1.orf.at/stories/476169 (Version: August 2016), German only

Particularly as just over a month after my disappearance the police had announced that we had to expect the worst and that my remains would surely be discovered one day. I think my parents were the only ones who could not reconcile themselves to that thought. Perhaps out of pure fear, perhaps because they truly - each of them in their own way - believed unfailingly that I would come back.

At the police station in Deutsch-Wagram I repeatedly said in any case, "Please do not alert the press yet. Give me some time to process all of this." I don't know whether the officers at the time thought that I was making myself overly important, or whether they simply underestimated what was happening. "Come on, girl. Stop your worrying now. The press isn't going to get in here!" As if the police station were on Mars and had become dislocated from the space-time continuum.

In fact, there was a sea of people out in front of the police station. Standing shoulder to shoulder, the reporters elbowed each other, pushing and shoving to get the best spots. One look out the window at the end of my first round of questioning finally made it crystal clear to every last police officer that there was no way I could stay there. But – where was I to go? Several telephone calls later the decision was made to transfer me to the building, where the Vienna Criminal Police Office was once located, for the time being. The building allowed for vehicle access through a courtyard and had corridors and rooms that could be cordoned off as necessary. This was unlike a normal police station, which needed to continue its day-to-day operations. However, the question was how I was supposed to leave the police station in the first place. There was no back door, no street that provided an alternative route into the city.

The answer came in the shape of a blue blanket the officers usually used if they had to spend the night at the station on call. In a way, this blanket brought me full circle. Once we had arrived at his parents' house at Heinestraße 60 in Strasshof, the kidnapper had also thrown a blue blanket over my head before dragging me from the van and placing me in the underground dungeon. The first few hours after my kidnapping, that blanket was the only thing I had with me underground. There was no mattress, no light. I could see nothing, hear nothing, except for the blood swishing through my veins. I felt the narrowness, the coldness, the bare floor. It smelled mouldy and like stale, warm, moist air that settled on me like a film and evoked a feeling of disgust. I was terribly afraid, and it took me an eternity until I dared free myself from the blue blanket. Finally, I rolled myself up in it, whimpering, when any feeling of time was long gone. Even though I tried so hard and kept telling myself, "Concentrate. Count. You have to count. Use your fingers and keep the passage of time in your memory." An attempt to impose structure on eternity.

What is time? What is time in captivity? Does it last a couple of hours, a day, a week, a month, a year? I think that if I had known that it would last for 3,096 days, I would've gone crazy. If I had known how massive my underground prison was and how cleverly the kidnapper had secured my hiding place, I might have given up much sooner. I might not have held on to the end. The fear of what would happen if he did not come down one day. The fear of dying of hunger, of thirst, and of being found as mummified remains purely by chance decades later was not something I felt on the first, or the second or even on the third day. Back then I still hoped that he would come to his senses, and that I would go free after the ransom was paid or following a heroic police rescue. After that, fear was my constant companion. In my first night I had no clue about any of that. I had only that blue blanket that gave me some warmth and protection.

Now I needed a blanket in order to take just a few steps from the police station to the car, wedged in between two police officers. Once we stepped outside, the cameras sprang into action. People called out loudly in the chaos, "A picture!" "A quick interview." Again and again calling out my name that I hadn't heard for so long, "Natascha, Natascha!"

The car took me to Vienna. The clicking of the cameras and the bright lights of the harsh camera flash hounded me for days. During one of my first weeks at the Vienna General Hospital there was a severe electrical storm one night. I was afraid to open my eyes, because I was certain that the photographers were standing around my bed, never ceasing to take pictures.

When the car arrived in front of the former Criminal Police Office, journalists were already gathered around the main entrance. Apparently this next step had also somehow been leaked. But we entered the building from the rear entrance, without anyone being able to take any more photographs of me.

The first person to do so was a construction worker at the hospital. A snapshot taken using his mobile phone, shot between a cup of coffee and a plate of kolatschen* pastries. I was with the social worker who had been assigned to me several days prior to that. We had gone down to the cafeteria for a moment. The picture was completely blurry, and I was fortunately unrecognizable. But the newspapers printed it anyway. The same goes for an interview "with me" that appeared in an Austrian magazine one week after my escape despite me having never made a statement of any kind to the publication in question. The eye-catcher was a picture stemming from a computer-generated photograph that had been used by the police to search for me. The data from the original missing persons photo had been combined with pictures of my parents when they were young in order to get some kind of idea of what I could have grown to look like.

The thirty-page article also showed sketches of my underground dungeon, reported about my life in the "house of horrors" and with "Mr. Strange". All of it was supported by quotes that I had never expressed either in that way or had made either during my initial questioning by police or during my interview with the police psychologist. A young female police officer who was the first person I told my story to in rough

---

* Small round pastries made with yeast dough and with poppy seeds, cream cheese and/or plum jam filling.

outlines had caved to the pressure after just a few hours. Untrained in how to deal with the media, relatively new to her job, in the end nobody protected her either.

Later a media researcher said that my "case" was the first in which the comparatively disciplined Austrian and German media had dropped any semblance of restraint. It wasn't until later on that it became clear just how right he was and just how much the politicians, the representatives of the judiciary and many a self-appointed investigator could, in good conscience, be lumped in with the media.

Even the police officers who had been tasked with establishing my identity had come under massive pressure. They were offered astronomical amounts of money for a photograph from the police station. Anyone who had anything to do with me either at the hospital or anywhere else, or had any connection to me, above all my parents and my relatives, was literally besieged. A counsellor from Vienna's psychosocial service was intercepted one evening in front of the hospital by a journalist, who said "Photograph? I can give you € 70,000 right now, cash in hand." He turned him down.

Although everybody was trying their level best to keep me away from the insanity raging outside as much as possible, I was aware of more than enough of it. To all of those who say that I decided to step out into the public spotlight either entirely of my own free will or even to satisfy my "craving for media attention", as many accused me of again and again later on, let me be clear that the situation at the time offered very little margin for manoeuvre. Efforts to "chase me down" would not have been tenable either for me or for my family, or for my advisors and the investigators over the long-term. The most farfetched guesses as to the details of my abduction and captivity were already being sold as facts, and the pressure weighing on everybody was enormous.

Added to this was the fact that I was repeatedly and regularly questioned by police during my first several days in the hospital. Again and again I tried to emotionally come to terms with my ordeal in the past.

And at the same time with what lie ahead in the future. I met with the legal expert who had been appointed to me by the Vienna Municipal Department of Youth and Family to discuss privacy protections, dealing with the media and my future. After he threw in the towel, my meetings were continued with the attorneys from a law firm that had a great deal of experience in dealing with the media and primarily with protecting victims.

Once we hired the law firm, I was constantly caught between competing approaches. On one hand with the doctors who saw me as a victim, a patient or even to some extent a research object and wanted to go public with me as such sooner or later; and on the other hand there were those whose job it was to develop a strategy to keep me away from that same public for as long as possible. One or two of the doctors even viewed the attorneys as part of the public, because they came from the outside. Just the fact that they had to be in contact with me, in order to evaluate me and to develop a strategy, gave rise to many a discussion. The everyday workings of the hospital must not be disturbed, which was understandable, and any kind of additional strain on me was to be avoided anyway, they said. Also understandable. But it was still kind of like trying to square the circle.

A few minutes after the first meeting with my new attorneys began in my room, a psychologist came in. At first the attorneys thought that she just had a question, and they interrupted their meeting with me. But she pulled up a chair and sat down. She said that it was her job to know what was being discussed here, as I was traumatized and had to be treated with the necessary caution. That was certainly correct, but somehow we had to move on from there. And of course there are issues that are essentially subject to confidentiality. One of my attorneys informed her that confidentiality was respected even in maximum-security prisons housing dangerous criminals. And I was here of my own accord. Aside from that, they were all on the same team, working toward the same goal, namely to make sure that no further damage was inflicted on me. In the end she left the room, but the fissures between the two sides remained. They eyed each other with mistrust, and I was caught in the middle, just like my parents who had very little understanding that they were being kept from me as much as possible – so as not to agitate me any further.

Early on my mother had attracted the attending physicians' anger when she complained that her child was being taken from her for a second time. Immediately after our brief reunion at the Criminal Police Office I was taken into so-called protective custody and taken to the province of Burgenland. At the time it was yet unclear what happened with the kidnapper. For my own protection I was taken to a strictly isolated hotel accompanied by a police psychologist. Arriving after a long drive, I was still very wound up and tense at the same time. I wondered what was happening in the search for the kidnapper and if he had been captured alive. Nobody would give me a straight answer when I asked about him.

The psychologist talked to me throughout the entire trip there, telling me about her holidays in Greece and Italy, evidently in an attempt to distract me. She wouldn't even stop talking at the hotel, where we had to share not only a room, but even a double bed. I kept imagining to myself that she had an off switch and I could shut down the avalanche of words at the touch of a button. I wanted to collect my thoughts, have some peace and quiet and primarily turn on the radio in order to finally know what had happened to the kidnapper. That wouldn't be good for me, as I needed to get some distance, I was told. Actually at that moment it would've been the first enormous step toward gaining distance if I had been able to find out that my ordeal was really over – one way or another.

Instead, she insisted that I finally eat something. Another officer went to get hamburgers and chips from McDonald's. The smell of the grease alone turned my stomach. After just a few bytes I pushed my food side and asked for chamomile tea. It was much easier on my stomach.

When she was done eating, I asked if I could take my first unmonitored bath in years. I had barely sat down in the tub when she began knocking at the door asking if everything was okay. Yes, yes, I answered.

Barely five minutes later she was knocking again, asking when I would be finished, if everything was really okay. After the third time she knocked I told her that I was not in the process of committing suicide, but merely wished to take a bath.

That night neither of us hardly slept a wink. She didn't because she wanted to keep an eye on me, and I didn't because being so close to somebody I didn't know was very uncomfortable. Today I can laugh at such an absurd situation, but at the time my feelings were in turmoil.

The next day, as we were driving back to Vienna, somebody told me that the kidnapper had killed himself. After yet another round of questioning, I was taken to the Vienna General Hospital. My mother was not informed until two days later, after a number of telephone calls. She was told that her daughter was traumatized and was undergoing examinations by medical experts, completely isolated from the outside world. The gentlemen themselves, who my mother thought had primarily clinical coldness and medical questionnaires to offer, not the emotions of a mother, were constantly appearing on her television screen. Everybody had something to say, although nobody was actually supposed to say anything. When my mother vented her anger, demanding to know why she was being kept from me, she received a call from the hospital, saying that she had better refrain from taking such unilateral steps in the future.

*

Further questioning by police took place in a small room on the basement level of the hospital from them on. Grey concrete, a number of tables and chairs, artificial light. The discussions with my attorneys were also moved to that room, because they were now "banned from the floor", whether it was due to the incident with the "curious" psychologist or in an attempt not to overly impact the daily operations of the hospital.

The main issue of our discussions was always the media. I had asked my attorneys to bring me a copy of Austrian legislation governing the media, but I was so exhausted that I had difficulty concentrating. The light hurt my eyes, my head swam, and it was all too much for me to take in.

Cautiously I was informed that "the whole world wanted to talk to me". After a meeting with me that lasted perhaps an hour, one of my attorneys received 55 new messages. Voicemail, e-mails, from countries such as Russia, Brazil, even New Zealand. The pressure was enormous, and everybody who was involved with my situation was under the microscope, being scrutinized by the global public. Speculation about my time in captivity ran wild. Five days after my escape, at a press conference on 28 August 2006, Dr. Friedrich read out a letter intended to answer the initial, most pressing questions, as well as to request a more moderate approach:

*"Dear journalists, reporters, dear world public,*
*I am very much aware of how strong an impression the events of the last several days must have made on all of you. I can well imagine how shocked and frightening it is to think that something like this is even possible. Furthermore, I am aware that you are somewhat curious about me and would naturally like to know more details about the circumstances under which I lived. However, allow me to first state that I do not want to and will not answer any questions concerning intimate or personal details. I will call out any attempts to violate my personal boundaries no matter who violates these boundaries in a voyeuristic way. Anyone attempting to do so will be in for a surprise. I have grown into a young lady with an interest in education and in human needs.*
*The room I lived in: My room was sufficiently furnished. It was my room. And not meant to be shown to the public.*
*My daily life: My daily routine followed a particular schedule. We would most often eat breakfast together, as he did not have to go*

*to work most of the time. Housework, reading, television, talking, cooking. That was it, for years on end. Everything was tied into fears of loneliness.*

*On my relationship: He was not my lord or master. I was just as strong as he was, but - symbolically speaking – I was carried in his arms and trampled underfoot. However, he – and he and I knew it – picked the wrong one to mess with.*

*He was the only one behind the kidnapping, and everything had already been prepared. Together with me, he set up and furnished the room, which was not only (?) 1.60 meters high. By the way, I did not cry after I escaped. There was no reason to be sad. In my eyes his death was unnecessary. Surely his punishment would not have meant the end of the world. He was a part of my life. That is why I do mourn him after a fashion. Of course it is true that my teenage years were quite different from those of many others. But essentially it is not my feeling that I have missed out. I was spared many an experience, such as trying alcohol and cigarettes, and having friends who were a bad influence on me.*

*Message to the media: The only aspect the press should spare me are the constant slanderous accusations levelled against me, the erroneous interpretations, know-it-all attitudes and the lack of respect shown to me.*

*At present I feel comfortable and safe where I am, albeit somewhat deprived of agency. But I have decided only to contact my family by telephone. I will decide for myself when I will contact journalists.*

*On my escape: When I was cleaning out the car in the yard and using the vacuum cleaner, he moved away from me as the vacuum cleaner was making so much noise. That was my opportunity, and I simply left the vacuum cleaner on.*

*By the way, I never called him "Lord" although he wanted me to. I think he wanted me to call him that, but he wasn't really serious. I have an attorney that I trust who is organizing the legal aspects* *of my situation together with me. Youth Ombudsperson Pinterits is a person I have taken into my confidence, and I am able to talk comfortably to Dr. Friedrich and Dr. Berger. The team led by Mr. Frühstück\* has been very good to me. I would like to express my friendly greetings to them, but they were indeed a bit curious. To be sure, that is what they do for living.*

*Intimate questions: Everybody always wants to ask intimate questions that are nobody's business. Perhaps I will tell a therapist some day, or somebody if I have the need to, or maybe never. This intimate knowledge belongs to me alone.*

*Mr. Ernst H\*\*– this is my message – should not feel guilty. He cannot help it, as it was Wolfgang's own decision to throw himself in front of the train. I feel empathy for Wolfgang's mother. I can put myself in their situation and feel what they must be feeling. The two of us and myself are thinking of him.*

*However I would like to thank all of those people who have expressed their empathy for my fate. Please allow me some peace and quiet in the upcoming weeks and months. Dr. Friedrich will explain with this statement. Many people are taking care of me. Give me some time until I can give you a report myself.*

*Natascha Kampusch"*

There was a great deal of speculation about that letter. Dr. Friedrich had appeared on stage in public with a convoluted piece of handwriting. The shutters clicked, and the video cameras whirred. After the press conference graphologists analyzed close-ups of video and photographic images and declared that the handwriting was not consistent with the handwriting of a young woman. Deletions and corrections could be seen in

---

\* Johann Frühstück was the chief investigator at the time.
\*\* Ernst H - friend of Wolfgang Priklopil's, who gave the kidnapper a ride in his car shortly before his suicide and later was caught in the crosshairs of the investigation.

the script. It is correct that the lines Dr. Friedrich read out had not been taken down in my handwriting, but rather in his. It is also correct that I felt the need to compose this appeal to the public. I had been allowed to sit at the computer in the nurse's room to put a few lines to paper. It is also correct that many of the statements that were made in my "letter to the world public" originated from my thoughts. But also from the talks that I had had with Dr. Friedrich.

Despite the enormous time pressures of the upcoming press conference, Dr. Friedrich absolutely insisted on copying out my words by hand – and "lending a hand" here and there, as he admitted, or in other words was forced to admit, to the media later on[*].

The scorn that was heaped on him afterwards was certainly not correct. However, his handling of the words that I had written myself or had entrusted to him was also not correct. The greatest difficulty for me came later, as the letter had built up expectations that I could only fail to meet. As a result a certain kind of poise and aptitude for analytical thought and serenity were attributed to me that I do possess in a way. I am analytical and clear-headed and aware of both my situation and the situation at large, because I would not have survived without those skills. I attach importance to nuances because if I had been unable to perceive the varied shades between black and white I would have given into despair, feeling only hate and anger for the kidnapper. But of course I live my life between a victim's two extremes of strength and weakness.

These two extremes are very far apart. At times I was all of that, and at times I wasn't. Because with everything that I had experienced in my very recent past, I had come from a position of strength and survival, and a victim would never characterize him or herself as such, because it would make the kidnapper powerful, or subsequently legitimize his position after the fact.

---

[*] http://www.sueddeutsche.de/panorama/betreuung-von-natascha-kampusch-schwieriger-auf-trag-1.859314 (Version: August 2016, German only)

Still, I was a young, vulnerable woman, a little girl who had been through hell. It took a while for me to allow people to see myself this way. Today I can show this side of me to a small circle of the people closest to me, and I can even talk about this dark, painful side in a protected space. About what it's like to process my memories so that they do not weigh on me and hurt me permanently. And yet, even today it is extremely rare for people to see me cry in public or break down in sobs. I handle those feelings in private. But that doesn't mean that I don't experience such moments. Even today I have problems defining my terrible experiences to myself. I don't mean to say in the least that nobody could understand me if I were to speak openly about my feelings. But for some things there are simply no words and no definitions. And I don't want to burden anybody with something that they perhaps are unable to shoulder. It may sound strange, but for me it has to do with the respect I have for others and with dignity.

2

# *"Ms. Kampusch, how are you?"*

## *The Interview*

The crime perpetrated against me, for whatever motives,
was a crime against many people. He inflicted trauma
on an entire society, throwing it off balance. Because
evil did in fact come along in the shape of a person you
would find to be perfectly ordinary.

That letter was the foundation of an image that is held against me even
today. What was still interpreted in the beginning as my unbelievable
strength, earning me nothing more like respect and a certain admiration,
turned against me as time went on. People had expected a kind of "Kas-
par Hauser"* figure, somebody who divided the world into black and
white, in good and evil. Somebody who tended to express herself rather
woodenly, just as people later suspected the children from Amstetten to

---

* A young man from Germany (1812?-1833) who claimed to have grown up in the total isolation of a darkened cell. https://en.wikipedia.org/wiki/Kaspar_Hauser

46

be able to speak only in grunts and hisses. A person, broken down from everything that had been done to her. And I was, of course. But I had not shattered during all my years in captivity, otherwise I would not have survived. I made a pact with my older self, who was to help me escape one day.

The sad thing is that I have been criticized for my actual "strength" or the "strength" that was visible on the outside. That people confused my reticence with "hiding something". And failed to make the effort to differentiate, to look below the surface. Instead, I was increasingly confronted with opinions, such as, "Anyone who talks like her, who views her situation in such a nuanced way, could not have suffered enough."

In the end, that letter, which was well intentioned by everybody and at the time was correct and expressed matters important to me in many areas, laid the foundation for exactly this perception of me.

In keeping with my metaphor, a couple days later I built the "first floor" on top of that foundation myself. The letter did not achieve its intended goal in the public, namely for me to have some peace and quiet. Just the opposite happened. The request to give me time until I was able to explain myself in more detail fell on deaf ears. What I had briefly revealed from my everyday life in captivity, and primarily what I had thought had not (yet) been disseminated in public simply fanned the flames of curiosity even higher. Media outlets were constantly trying to outbid each other to be the first to get an interview. The US was the only country with a strangely reluctant request – at least from one newspaper: "OK, a girl was locked in some basement by a madman in Vienna for eight and a half years, and everybody wants to talk to her. But can you tell me once again what the story is?"

That was the story. In essence. That request from the US was, looking back, a warning that it was not going to be enough. That the story would take on a life of its own, that the gaps the public believed it had a right to fill had to be filled. And if I were unwilling to fill them, then other people would do it for me. Then their imagination and fantasies of what had happened in the intervening years would be the ones people remembered. As if people could not allow actual events to stand on their own, as if they had to attach something more to them, making them even uglier, more disgusting, more unpalatable.

This is the kind of exaggeration that I described above, that apparently makes it easier to hold a crime like this at arm's length. The moment when it exceeds every value benchmark, every norm, we feel we no longer have to doubt or re-examine our own values and norms.

It took me some time to understand these mechanisms. I myself did not have this artificial space between me and the crime. For me it was not an abstraction of cruelty beyond anyone's ability to imagine. For me it was something I lived every day. I could not understand why people were looking for further revelations. Very quickly it was no longer about verification and facts, but about new speculations one after the other, and bigger and juicier headlines in order to drive up circulation numbers. It is sad to see how far some media outlets will go – even today. How they willingly ignore the consequences or even exploit them for their next sensationalist cover. First they signal the hunt is on and then, somewhat later, hypocritically admonish others to leave the girl in peace already. She can hardly set one foot outside the door, the poor dear.

Looking back I asked myself again and again whether it was the right thing to do to provide the public with the information the way I did. I had no influence on anything that was leaked or planted in a targeted way. I do not regret that I sat down in front of the camera and spoke for myself, even though I had only a limited impact on when that took place. I had wanted my freedom, and that also included my freedom to express myself. Despite my efforts, exactly what I was trying to avoid ended up happening anyway.

Everything that was left unsaid in my first three interviews, because I was not yet able or willing to talk about it, was later used against me. As if I had purposely wanted to keep something secret. Either to avoid having to reveal the entirety of the horror or to mask that the whole thing

48

hadn't really been that bad after all.

By stepping into the public spotlight, in a way I lost control of my own story. Other people took control of it, interpreting it, falsifying it, interpreting and evaluating me and my behaviour against their own expectations. They couldn't just be content to let me be me, and they couldn't allow my experiences to be what they were. As a result, I was once again transformed into an object, into a projection screen for the thoughts and imaginations of others. That was exactly what I was in captivity. A kind of modelling clay, supposedly malleable, able to be shaped according to the wishes of the kidnapper who believed that he could in his own small way play God. On the outside, I became the same modelling clay once again.

I didn't want to have to live up to expectations, to go along with how other people wanted me to be. I just wanted to be me. Freedom implies for me permission to be where I want to be, to say what I want to say and to keep silent about what I don't want to say. But that is apparently an understanding of freedom that many have a problem with.

In the beginning I suddenly was the victim of the nation that people wanted, felt they had to help. It was like an occupying force. All around me, my family, the advisors, attorneys and psychiatrists. Caregivers who monitored when I slept, what I ate. Who offered me pills so that I could finally get on a normal day-night cycle. Doctors who wanted to give orders about which questions the investigators would be allowed to ask and who would be allowed to see me and when. Out in front of the hospital, the paparazzi, on the newspaper stands at the kiosk downstairs the brightly coloured publications with their at times well-meaning, concerned headlines, and at other times sensationalistic speculations about intimate details.

*

After the pressure increased yet again as a result of the press conference, my team of advisors decided that I should address the public myself by giving one or several interviews as soon as possible. My corresponding interview partners would also be selected "according to medical criteria". In other words, taking into account a certain level of integrity that was to be expected with regard to protecting me as a victim and protecting my privacy. This was to prevent any re-traumatization. They were to be three interviews: one with Austria's largest newspaper in terms of circulation, the Kronen-Zeitung, one with the magazine News and a TV interview with the Austrian Broadcasting Corporation (ORF).

Innumerable requests had come from Germany, mainly from private commercial broadcasters. Many in the press were speculating that up to € 1 million had been offered for an exclusive interview on television. I don't know whether those numbers are correct, and in the end it didn't matter to me anyway. I wanted a framework that allowed me to feel comfortable, inasmuch as that was possible. I wanted to be taken seriously and treated with respect, and I did not want to be used to drive ratings, wedged in between the report about cosmetic surgery and Ballermann*.

A room at the Vienna General Hospital was remade into a comfortable studio for the ORF interview. The television viewers were not supposed to see right away that I was staying in the hospital. The broadcaster sent 30 people to the interview, making it into an enormous affair. The camera operators were women, and everything was bathed in a soft light. A blue-grey carpet was laid down in the otherwise rather austere room, a cream coloured cabinet was set up and a number of green plants dotted the room. A living room atmosphere with two light-coloured leather chairs, each with a side table with small table lamps and books. Next to my chair was a stack of colourful pillows. That was the only thing that I had asked for, aside from a package of Kleenex tissues. The tissues in case I felt the need to cry, and a pillow in case I needed to hold tight to

---

* Party at the biggest, most famous area on Mallorca

something. Neither of them was necessary. But I liked one of the pillows so much that I was allowed to keep it as a souvenir.

Everybody was extremely tense in the hours leading up to the interview. That afternoon we role-played the interview situation briefly. "So that you won't be startled by everything later on," as one of my advisors put it. Then the makeup team went to work on me in my hospital room, with doctors' orders to make me look "as natural as possible".

Then we went downstairs into the "hospital studio". In the corridor I met Christoph Feurstein for the first time who was to conduct the interview. In the last eight and half years since my disappearance he had reported on my case on numerous occasions. It's probably not an assignment that journalists are usually clamouring for, namely to knock on doors and ask for interviews with family members still suffering from the loss or the disappearance of a loved one. Two days after my kidnapping, he visited my mother for the first time at our flat at Rennbahnweg. After that, his desk reported on my case every year on 2 March, the day of my disappearance. And every time that there were supposedly new developments, dead ends that the investigators had run up against, or every time somebody reported to have seen me somewhere, or claimed to have information that "would lead to my discovery".

Years later Christoph Feurstein told me that he was the youngest journalist on the team for the news magazine Thema and it simply "fell to him" to have to ask about the feelings and fears that my mother felt those first few hours and days after my disappearance. And also because his reporting had made him feel a special kinship with "difficult stories". He had never followed a family for such a long time, particularly as the story never really went anywhere, he says. There was nothing to report over the years that would have constituted a serious contribution toward solving my case. Nothing seemed to turn out for the better; it was always the same tragic situation. Stagnation. He said that my parents' grasping at every straw was what upset him the most. On one hand, the small-scale war waged by the former couple, on the other hand their unified stance in declaring that if I were no longer alive, they would no longer have any reason to live. The interviews that Christoph conducted with my parents during my captivity were also used as visual evidence for the doctors who were now treating me. They form the basis for the psychological assessments aimed at clarifying whether and to what extent first my parents had perhaps abused me, second whether my childhood had been miserable and I could have simply run away, and third if they could've had anything to do with my kidnapping in any way.

When it was clear that the ORF was to carry out and broadcast the exclusive interview, it was also clear who my interview partner would be. The questions were roughly coordinated with me and my doctors in terms of content. But still, nobody knew how I would react when it came down to it. We also agreed that I could take brief breaks from recording – not least due to my cold and my hoarse voice. It was even agreed that it would be possible to suspend the interview if the attending doctors were of the opinion that I was not able to handle the whole situation. It would've been a problem not only for the ORF, but also my team of advisors would likely have been the target of massive criticism if I had been unable to withstand the pressure.

Christoph had a preliminary meeting with the psychiatrists, who told him that I was surprisingly eloquent and a strong young woman, and that the trauma I had suffered would likely only become fully visible and comprehensible over time. He didn't know any more than that. It was certainly unusual that we did not have a meet-and-greet before the interview, and that he was unable to get a feel for me, his interview partner. I wasn't able to get a feel for things either. It was like jumping into the deep end for everybody.

We briefly said hello and then went to our respective chairs.

*"Over the last several days so many people have been asking me how you are doing. And it is unbelievable that you are sitting here now and that I can ask you myself. Ms. Kampusch, how are you?"*

"Mh, yes. Good, con… considering the circumstances."

*"You have now been free for two weeks. How have you experienced your newfound freedom. What have you been up to?"*

"Well, primarily I am trying to recover from the exertions of my escape, to relax. (…)"

*"Who are the people that you are talking to most right now, that you trust the most?"*

"Yes, well, the ones I trust the most, hm. Dr. Friedrich, for example, but also all of the psychologists who are taking care of me. And mainly I really trust my whole family. And of course I trust in myself."

After the interview a survey was carried out asking people what they thought of the interview and what they wished for me. A total of 98 percent said they wished me all the best and hoped that I would now be left alone in order to prepare for my new life.

Shortly thereafter public opinion changed completely after the German news magazine Stern reported that I had gone skiing with the kidnapper. At the time I had denied it even though it was the truth, albeit a very abbreviated version of the truth. Because it did not reflect the very complex kidnapper-victim relationship that had developed over the years in which a ski trip shortly before my 18th birthday was in no way a pleasure outing, but rather a tool with which to show me just how much of a nobody I was and how far Priklopil could project his power. During our trip to the Hochkar ski resort I had tried to attract the attention of a woman I encountered in the toilet of the ski lodge. After I had gathered up all of my courage, nothing more than an inconsequential peep came out of my mouth. The woman smiled at me in a friendly way and walked through the door where the kidnapper was already waiting impatiently for me.

I have been asked over and over why I was unable to or did not escape sooner. And, as I've already pointed out, over and over again people suspected me of staying with him voluntarily. These are accusations that heap scorn on what I have experienced. In order to make everything easier for observers on the outside to cope with? I don't know.

Every step I took was carefully monitored and controlled by the kidnapper. I was weighed, and the food I ate and the air I breathed were rationed. I had to beg to be given attention in any shape or form – be it in the shape of a book or an audio cassette. Any misbehaviour from the perspective of the kidnapper was punished. And when he was upstairs in the house, his voice boomed through the intercom into my dungeon, "Obey!"

Over the years he gradually increased his threats and intimidations of me. He claimed that he would kill the neighbours who happened to hear my voice while I was working in the house. And then I would never see the light of day again. After many years, whenever I drove with him to a DIY outlet or some other shop for the first time, he would show me out in front of the driveway what he planned to do if I made a false move. "Look, I can use that to slice open your carotid artery." Or, "I can use that to beat your skull in. Nobody would be quick enough to stop me."

Once a journalist actually asked me why I believed everything he said. It really is quite obvious that anyone who is ready and willing to kidnap a child and to lock her in a windowless basement dungeon for years is capable of anything. Sometimes I got tired of answering questions like that. On one hand the need for embellishment and horror and on the other hand the naïveté, the refusal or inability to imagine that some things truly go beyond anyone's comprehension, is not something you can blame anyone for. But I would have liked for someone to at least try to grapple with the concept that there is such a thing as an internal and external prison.

My external prison was in place from the very beginning, while my internal prison was constructed over the ensuing years. Priklopil knew all too well how to paint the world outside as a nest of terror. He was my protector and nobody else. He was my rescuer, the only one I meant anything to, nobody else. The only one who took care of me when everybody else had long ago turned their backs on me. Even the police, who were now only searching for my remains.

One of the worst scenes during the last several years of my captivity was when he shoved me, wearing only a pair of panties, half-starved, covered in bruises and with my head completely shorn, in front of the front door and said, "Come on now, run. Let's see how far you get." I was so humiliated and filled with shame that I couldn't take a single step. He tore me away from the door, saying, "So you see. The world out there doesn't want you anyway. Your place is here and only here."

Immediately after my escape, the psychiatrists were of the opinion that the complex kidnapper-victim relationship, which had developed over all those years between Priklopil and myself, could not be summed up in just a few short sentences. They said that it would be difficult for people to comprehend that my internal prison had grown much stronger than my external one over time. That people felt the need for simple solutions and simple explanations, even though such a thing was de facto impossible in my case. What we didn't realize at the time was that with a story of these dimensions nothing can be kept secret. However, at the time some things were not included in the narrative for good reason. But when they were made public, I was punished.

In the minds of many our "ski holiday" was the symbol that supposedly relativized my time in captivity. However, just the opposite was the case. This episode demonstrated nothing more than the extent of my internal prison. Just how deeply I had internalized the kidnapper's threats. Just how omnipresent he was at all times of the day and night. And at the same time how difficult it is to penetrate this interwoven mesh of dependency, power and its abuse and to make it comprehensible to the public.

\*

The next step in my new life began with a change of address. I no longer wanted to stay in the hospital. The most important examinations had been completed, and I wanted out.

On 7 September 2006 I wrote in my diary:

*Everybody was satisfied, with me and with the interview as well. I couldn't really tell how I'm doing myself. I wanted to find out and I requested permission to leave. Dr. M. let me go through what looked like a cable duct to the back door of the hospital. All of a sudden I was confronted with kerbs, pavement stones, ramps and pedestrian crossings. Moreover, people were coming toward me on the sidewalk. Some whispered to each other or turned around. I tried to concentrate on taking every single step.*
*I tried to buy a straw hat on Alserstrasse, but nobody was there. In another shop I discovered a knitted hat as well as a pink purse. The saleslady watched me with her mouth hanging open. But it wasn't until a customer walked in that I was recognized and the knowledge of my identity was shared in a whisper. I left that shop very quickly. When I went to get ice cream with Dr. Berger just a few days after my escape, nobody recognized me. I wonder what exactly things will be like in the future.*

Everybody was concerned about my future. If the doctors had had their way, I would have remained in the hospital. If the attorneys had had their way, I was to hang out with other young people as much as possible in order to recapture my lost youth somewhat. An initial evening outing to Vienna's "bar scene" with a couple of young employees from my attorneys' firm simply ended up in heightening tensions among "my advisors". The doorman did not want to let me into the hospital due to the late hour, citing a potential violation of hospital rules. And the next day, I received a scolding.

I was in the hospital voluntarily, not because I posed a danger to myself or others. I had been examined, and there was no reason for me to extend my stay. I wanted to live in my own home, and not in a sterile room with hospital furniture. My wish was not met with unmitigated support. If I left now, I needn't think that I could come back, I was told. That meant the next pillar of my team had crumbled. When I packed my bag, many of the comments were truly not very well-intentioned, "Oh, leaving so soon? I suppose you're all better already?"

A nurses' residence at Rosenhügel in Vienna's 13th district was offered up as an interim solution. A small, 19 square-metre flat on the 11th floor. When I moved in at the end of September, not even five weeks after I escaped, I had to sign a paper promising not to jump out of the window. Other methods of committing suicide went unconsidered.

I borrowed some furniture, including two tables. Even after such a short time, letters and printouts of emails ended up being stacked on one of those tables. I would like to take this opportunity to thank from the bottom of my heart all of those who offered me courage back then. It gave me a great deal of strength to see that people felt empathy with me and understanding for my situation. Often it was parents who wrote me encouraging words describing their kind-hearted feelings, telling me how much my story had moved them and how happy they were they and their children had never met with a similar fate. Older people, who had experienced terrible things, not only during the war, and saw themselves reflected in my story to some degree; they knew what it felt like to have survived. I also received autobiographical accounts, written mainly by women who had experienced traumatic events in their childhoods or adolescence and some of whom were still in therapy. Many saw parallels between their fate and mine and wanted to offer me support, or perhaps hoped to receive support from me.

In addition to all of these positive or even moving letters, just as many letters were sent to me with very strange contents. The least of these were requests for autographs; the letters ran the entire gamut, ranging from offers of marriage to acting jobs and even invitations. Some wanted to go on a trip with me or send me on holiday. Others wanted to move into the kidnapper's house with me or offered me work in their homes. If I were to work diligently in the family business for a monthly board of € 57, we were certain to come to an agreement, they wrote. Mothers wrote on behalf of their sons, trying to highlight their positive characteristics as a future partner. A number of them wanted to adopt me, while others told me straight out which future role I was to play in life, pointing out that I had already learned how to be a slave. I received obscene photos and moral admonishments delivered for free to my house, including several Bibles and other types of uplifting literature.

In the very beginning I was inundated with chocolate, flowers and small gifts. Over the years I have received various talismans and other good luck charms, as well as homemade jewellery made with "energetic stones" by people who said they wanted to offer me mental support. Little girls have sent me poems and drawings, and utter strangers sent me € 20, which I was supposed to use to make a wish come true. Artists have sent me their art work, mostly portraits of me, often stylized as angels or ethereal beings. However, there have also been stalkers who have repeatedly sent inappropriate letters, pictures and objects. Two of them, who were particularly persistent, were even ordered by the courts later on to maintain their distance from me and my family.

Again and again I receive letters from people requesting a new stove or Christmas presents for their children. Ominous aid organizations have asked for donations, while new age associations have asked me to share my "aura" with them in order to give "lost souls" strength. Yet others have seen me as the spawn of the devil, intending to destroy me so that I would be unable to use my destructive powers here on Earth any longer. They have quite openly blamed me for the death of the kidnapper, saying that he was my first victim. A strange reversal of our roles, which was not only promoted by such "crazies", but was later to become a part of my everyday life. I was being pilloried and had to justify my version of events. I was doubted, and even accused of lying. This was mostly when the newspapers once again reported on the "Kampusch case" or after I had given an interview.

The first few weeks and months of my freedom was like a balancing act, trying to figure out how to deal with all of these messages. The spectrum of emotions the messages expressed sometimes made me afraid. I had thought I had left possessiveness and psychotic fantasies behind me forever. I could hardly believe the comparatively large number of people who apparently desire to live like that every day. How many of them there were who identified with the kidnapper, who had managed to do something that they had likely always dreamed of.

These issues came up again and again in my talks with my psychologist. The danger of being re-traumatized, the fear of going out on the street and running into people there for whom just looking at me triggered an entire chain of perverse fantasies. In my dungeon I believed that only upstanding, interested and civilized people lived in the world outside, who respected every individual person and meant well by them. Naturally I really knew better, but compared to the kidnapper, the world seemed that way in my memories. Once I had escaped, I had the strangest experiences even in normal, everyday situations, such as in public transport or out shopping. It was a challenge to go out in public on a daily basis. But this was exactly the challenge I wanted to face. For a long time I accepted no compromise, and I wanted to move about freely just like everybody else. I actually managed to keep it up for around six years, then I slid into a phase where I hardly wanted to leave my house. I was constantly tense and under fire from the media, and it was often torture just taking one step outside my door. I couldn't take it anymore that some people stared at me so strangely. That teenagers laughed at me, that still others gave me reproachful or fearful looks.

All of that, but also coupled with some who did know how to keep their proper distance, by offering me spontaneous and well-intentioned hugs, making me nervous and embarrassing me. I didn't want to be noticed, I only wanted to be normal. But I have a sign on my forehead that says "victim of violence". Sometimes I am afraid that I can never be free to make the acquaintance of anyone again who does not have a preconceived opinion of me. When I'm older, maybe there will be people who no longer know my story, and for whom I am just one of many.

It was a mixture of defiance and masochism that I subjected myself to it for so long. Furthermore, I had been a spectator of life out there for long enough, and I no longer wanted to lock myself up. It was really bad when all of the investigations were opened up time and again, accompanied by the ghastliest speculations. Then some people would spit on the ground in front of me or hiss at me as I walked by, telling me that I should be ashamed of myself, that I was such a trollop, but that was no wonder considering my family.

I like to spend my time in a shop where you can buy stones and other materials for jewellery making, because making jewellery has meanwhile become a hobby of mine. One time I was there, standing at the cashier's desk, when a middle-aged woman accosted me, asking why I "had not stayed down there in my hole in the ground with a millstone around my neck instead of trying to dupe the world with my web of lies."

Most of the time I can manage to keep such behaviour at arm's length, when I remind myself that it's not really aimed at me personally, but at me as a slate for their own projections. Often erroneous interpretations or misunderstandings lead people to think poorly of me. However, sometimes it's simple cold-heartedness and hate. I don't always have to recognize and understand the underlying attitude, but I have to deal with it.

I wonder if the people who criticize me are themselves as thoughtful and irreproachable as they require me to be? As a result of my case in and of itself, in coming to terms with the crime, with my captivity and with how people and the media have treated me, I have seen and experienced things that remain hidden from others as a rule. Often people only see the supposedly beautiful surface and too often forget that underneath there is an interwoven network of uncontrollable urges and inconsistencies. This is where the human drive to put others down seems to belong. To put them in their place. My place is apparently not where I thought it was. In a certain way, I was not allowed to be free after all.

## 3

# *Getting Reacquainted*
# *under Intense Public Scrutiny*

### *My Parents, the Media and Me*

He told me, "You are not really here you know. You
were buried somewhere long ago. And your mother
killed you, and now they're all behind bars. Your father,
your mother and your entire family, because they were
all involved in your murder conspiracy."
It shocked me that out there similar ideas were circulat-
ing and my parents were under general suspicion.

The press hotly debated the question of why I did not move back in with
my parents after my long years of captivity. My parents had long ceased
to be a couple, and each of them had since built their own lives. My
father had a new partner, and my mother had her cats and her grand-
children, even though the media constantly suggested that she had other interests. She had still maintained my old room, where nothing had

been changed except for the colour of the walls. When I was kidnapped, the room was pink, and was now painted in a fresh green colour. All of my posters and pictures were still hanging on the wall, and the bed was still made up with my favourite sheets from before. Moreover, all of my stuffed animals were still sitting next to the pillow. All of the things that were important to me as a child were still stored in the grey display case: a silver Mercedes model car that my father had given me once, a garishly coloured Barbie horse that whinnied when you pressed its saddle. A mama bear with her cubs and the nature books by Ruth Thomson that I used to practice reading in the afternoons after coming home from grade school.

*Many different kinds of insects were buzzing and humming, worrying and swarming around the flowers. Among the insects was Tinchenbienchen. Tinchenbienchen lived in a hollow log together with thousands of other bees that were just as busy as she was. Tinchenbienchen was a little bit snooty and liked to leave the hive alone early in the morning. Once when the little bee came back, everybody had gone. Tinchenbienchen felt very lonely and started to look for the others. And there, next to an enormous blackberry bush was the entire beehive. "Finally," cheered Tinchenbienchen, "There they are!"*
*In her excitement she wasn't looking where she was going. She almost got caught up in a nearly invisible spider's web.\**

This was exactly the passage I read aloud for a feature story done by the Austrian Broadcasting Corporation (ORF) one year after my escape. I didn't plan it. I simply grabbed a book that was at hand, sat down on the floor, opened it and began to read. When I saw the broadcast later on,

---

\* Abridged text; In the original by Ruth Thomson: "The Story of Tinchenbienchen. My Book of Bees ", Readers Digest, Zurich 1988

it seemed like a parable for my past, and in a way the passage was fitting for my present situation as well.

*

While I was held captive it upset me to imagine what my parents must have felt after my disappearance. My mother most of all especially considering the quarrel we had just before I had left. "You must never part ways angry. You never know if you will see each other again!" That is one of the sayings that she taught me growing up. Just like, "An Indian knows no pain." I used her strength, which seemed unattainable to me as a child, because I believed I would never live up to her expectations, to buck myself up all those years in the dungeon when I felt emotionally downtrodden. As well as the knowledge that both of them loved me, even if they had not always expressed it the way I had hoped. That may be due to the fact that their generation never learned to display their emotions. A generation that itself grew up with significant hardship at a time when the focus was not on self-attainment, but rather on not acknowledging your personal needs.

In my family I was the baby of the family, born after my mother had gotten unexpectedly pregnant once more at the age of 38. My two half-sisters from her first marriage had already reached the age of adulthood. My mother certainly had not planned to get pregnant again, and I was seen more as a burden in a phase of my mother's life where she thought that everything would be getting easier again. She had had my two older sisters when she was very young and had raised them nearly all by herself, keeping her head above water with several jobs just to put food on the table. In addition to working as a seamstress, she later took over a small shop with an adjacent café together with my father. The year I was born a corner grocery store was added. My father delivered baked goods in his delivery van, and my mother took care of the rest. They didn't have much time for a small child.

Nevertheless, as the baby I was the centre of attention for a long time. My older sisters treated me like a little Miss Sunshine, pushing me around in the buggy and presenting me proudly to their friends. My father would romp through the flat with me when he wasn't working or out partying with friends. He liked to go out very much and often, and he was not somebody who was good at handling money, which made my mother furious. While she worked her fingers to the bone, he frittered their money away, piling up debts so high that his parents' bakery finally had to be seized.

For me, the bakery with its small shop, which hardly appeared to have changed over the decades, was the epitome of home. And the more my parents fought at home and the farther apart they grew from each other, and by extension from me, the more important my grandmother became. Her house in Süßenbrunn, an old village in the northern suburbs of Vienna, with numerous fruit trees in her garden, was a place where I felt happy. Running around in the garden, popping berries into my mouth, nicking a roll from the bakery, watching my grandmother cook in her flowered apron, I felt that everything was right with the world.

My own world, back in our council flat at Rennbahnweg, was in the process of unravelling. My parents were fighting more and more often, slamming doors, and the atmosphere was sombre. First they lost each other and the love they felt for one another, and now I was losing my place in a family that was continually drifting apart. I was five when my father moved out. There was nobody left to make me laugh, to toss his princess in the air and to play "giddy-up horsey" on his round belly. I took their separation badly, not understanding what had happened, and I wondered whether I was at least partly to blame. I had very little desire to go out, and I holed myself up in my room. And when I began kindergarten a bit later, I started wetting myself again. At first it was only at night, later on it was during the day.

It was the start of a very humiliating phase for me, where I lost every ounce of my self-esteem. My mother responded with hard-heartedness, incomprehension and desperation at my "problem", accusing me of doing it on purpose when everything else was already so difficult to deal with. It was my own fault if the other kids teased me, if the teachers embarrassed or punished me, she told me. When I complained, she mocked me for being "a delicate little flower", telling me that I had to toughen up, particularly towards myself. When I cried, she was particularly harsh. Sometimes she would slap me, telling me that at least then I would know why I was crying.

I felt neglected, worthless, small. I was no longer the fun-loving girl with the friendly smile, but rather a girl with sad eyes who tried to compensate for her despair and feelings of rejection with food. I ate and ate, gobbling up everything I could get my fingers on until my belly ached. At the age of 10 I was around 1.45 metres tall and weighed 45 kilos. What followed was even more ridicule, even more teasing, even more rejection. A vicious cycle that I could no longer escape.

A number of things that particularly upset me while in captivity arced back to my past. Controlling what I drank, for example. When I couldn't stop wetting the bed during my kindergarten years, every drop of fluid intake was strictly regulated. I wasn't allowed anything to drink before going to bed and only allowed to have a drink while out and about if a toilet was within reach. I was always thirsty. Later on, when I was trying to comfort myself with food, I downed sticky-sweet fizzy drinks by the litre. Nothing in moderation.

Down in the dungeon I sometimes thought I was suffocating because my tongue would stick to the roof of my mouth so thickly. I would go half crazy if I were given only a couple of dry cookies or zwieback to eat that I couldn't get down without any liquids. The kidnapper's voice on the intercom, barking at me, "Have you drunk everything up again?" Comments like, "Just look at yourself. You are fat and ugly." Before, my mother had sometimes said to me mockingly, "All you have to do is put an ugly girl in a pretty dress." All of that had buried itself deep in my soul, and now my wounds were being torn open again.

Later, when I started puberty, the kidnapper began to deprive me of food in a targeted way in order to weaken me, physically and mentally. I starved, at times for days on end, while every bite was strictly regulated. He would fish the hard-boiled eggs and sausage pieces out of the sausage salad that his mother sometimes made upstairs, and that I was given a portion of from time to time, so that only a couple of onions and toma-toes would be left swimming in the dressing.

After my parents divorced, I used food in an attempt to compensate for a lack of closeness and love. In the dungeon, food was the tool the kidnapper used to make me submit, to break me and to bind me to him. After the worst periods of food deprivation, I would be ecstatic when the kidnapper gave me a piece of cake. He was taking notice of me, I had ap-parently not made any mistakes, and I received affection by way of food.

In my family food had always played a significant role. We never went on an outing without stopping to eat somewhere, and no family celebration was complete without a richly set table with dumplings and a roast, with cake for dessert. While my father got larger, my mother was able to eat an enormous amount of food without gaining as much as a single gram. When I began to gain weight so rapidly, she fluctuated between control and ignorance, saying, "Stop stuffing everything in your mouth." Most of the time, however, she was too busy to rap me on the knuckles, while I sat in a room adjacent to her shop, doing my home-work and continually munching on chocolate and other sweets.

However, the kidnapper was a man with a pronounced phobia of food, who forced his anorexic tendencies on me. When I was 16 I weighed only 38 kilos despite being 1.57 metres tall. Eating did not entail any kind of pleasure or joie de vivre for him, rather a bothersome duty or something that was tied to achievement. Only those who worked hard would earn a heel of bread. Even when I wanted a glass of water –

just because I was thirsty – it would end in a fight.

Only after inflicting severe abuse on me would he be comparatively generous. A couple of gummy bears, a piece of chocolate, a couple of cookies, a glass of milk. As if he wanted to ease his guilty conscience. Later when I knew that I could exercise some power of my own, it was one of my strategies to refuse to touch the treats. I wanted him to choke on his guilty conscience.

It was an attempt to pay him back somewhat and on a different level for the torture that he subjected me to on a daily basis. At no time did I forget that my entire survival depended on the kidnapper. I was as dependent on him as only small children are on their parents. I was used to following orders given by adults, even if I didn't understand the point of them. I understood the give-and-take between receiving attention and being ignored, and I had learned to be grateful even for small gestures. Children can adapt to the harshest circumstances. They are dependent and needy and will always try to see their way to viewing the positive side in even the cruellest person they have a close relationship with, as stunted as that positive side may be.

A lot of ink has been spilled on this subject after my escape. Many times people disregarded the fact that I simply had no other choice if I wanted to survive. Rather they claimed that I purportedly had had a romantic relationship with the kidnapper.

I do not know what the kidnapper saw in me. It was inevitable that the two of us had a connection, but it was certainly not a connection that was born out of love. Affection is not a feeling that coercion and enforced captivity can foster.

If anybody loved me, it was my parents, and in fact they still do today. It must've been like a slap in the face for them to be pilloried in the media and to read that I had a stronger connection to my torturer than to them. That I had stayed with him voluntarily to avoid having to return to my family that had been torn apart.

To all of those who believe that I would like to say that my family gave me many abilities that helped me survive my captivity. My mother taught me discipline and a certain ability to push emotions aside. My father taught me to imagine other worlds, alternative realities and to escape to them. Even if it was all just in my head. My grandmother gave me an emotional stockpile of comfort and warmth that I was able to think back to when I could no longer bear the cold and dark of my dungeon.

*

My parents did not deserve the treatment that they received both after my kidnapping and after my escape. I was a child of divorce like millions of others. My parents worked for a living, something that is more or less the norm nowadays. I was picked up and pampered one minute, and ignored and seen as a disruption the next, or treated as an unwilling pawn in their ongoing feud to denigrate each other and to build themselves up. Papa loves you more, because... Papa couldn't possibly love you as much as I do, because... This is an everyday occurrence for children whose parents have nothing more to say to each other, or are only able to engage in mutual recrimination.

You do not have to have grown up on the outskirts of Vienna, in one of these suburbs with no centre and no character, to have experienced what I did. Tower-like buildings housing council flats, designed on an architect's drawing board and plunked down on once lush expanses of green, interrupted every so often by shopping malls with brightly coloured light-up billboards. When the housing estate was built in the 1970s, the city planners likely patted each other on the back at how successful their residential vision-turned-reality appeared at first glance. A total of 2,400 generously apportioned, light-filled flats with balconies for over 7,000 people, who would pay good money for them, between park-like courtyards. When I was growing up there, there was very little left over from the estate's one-time glory. Rennbahnweg was seen as a socially depressed area with high unemployment. The atmosphere among the many residents was apathetic to openly aggressive. Many young people took drugs, and adults drank alcohol to numb their frustrations.

This was openly visible to everybody. It was easy to point the finger at "them" and tell yourself how lucky were not to live there. How lucky that you were different from those poor, hopeless people with their sad lives with no prospects. It is often overlooked that hopelessness, frustration and interpersonal problems existed just as often behind freshly painted façades, in affluent villas with tidy front yards, where father washes the car on Saturdays, and mother takes care of the home and children because one salary is enough.

This may sound somewhat cynical, but I experienced things in the house of just such a supposedly perfect family that I never could have imagined. I experienced how it is when the neighbours are content to say that the man in the house next door was always so nice, meticulous and polite, and always so proper. Nobody takes the time anymore to look behind the façade, assuming instead that everything is most likely in order.

The private life of my family was laid bare for public opprobrium, for the cliché hammer to come swinging down on it. What had happened to me and to them seemed all of a sudden to have been "expected". In 2009, when the second evaluation commission was formed – with the stated goal of clarifying internal investigation missteps – the negative images painted of my parents and my childhood reached an unprecedented apex. In a newspaper interview, the chairman of the commission disseminated his view that my time in captivity was possibly "undoubtedly better" than what I had "experienced prior to that". Considering the conditions under which I had grown up, it was not possible to seriously assume that I "just happened" to become a victim.* It was even possible

---

* Kronenzeitung, 4 August 2009

that everything was interconnected, that there was a link between the kidnapper and my parents. And if those suspicions were not confirmed, well it was also possible, after all, that I had consciously opted for the "alternative lifestyle solution" already mentioned, thankful to have finally escaped from the misery and wretchedness of home.

\*

When my parents received news that I had resurfaced, they must have been almost delirious with happiness. A period of time extending over eight years was condensed and shrunk into one single moment of reunion. Everything was burdened with too much emotion, hope, joy and uncertainty. Nobody knew how to deal with the situation. Added to this were expectations from others, as the press was already on the scene. How are people, who haven't seen each other for so long, supposed to behave? When you last saw someone as an elementary school kid, and are now standing across from an adult woman, who, in the intervening years, has experienced – well, what exactly?

The first meeting with my mother took place in the building formerly housing the Vienna Criminal Police Office. When the police car drove up, journalists tried to block access to the building through the back entrance. They beat on the roof of the car, pressing microphones and cameras against the windows. Just a few days after our first meeting, my mother described how it felt for her to go up into the building like this:

*"I walked into the building there, my heart starting to beat harder and harder, hammering harder and harder, and in the elevator I was already thinking to myself, that's the door. But it was just the elevator. Then I still had to wait a little while, but it was just crazy. I am so proud of my girl, that she managed to do it. So unbeliev-*

*ably proud and happy."*

Eight birthdays, eight Christmases and Easters, for eight years I had been waiting for this moment. For eight years I had been longing for a loving word, a touch from my mother. When that moment had finally come, I didn't know how to handle it. My happiness was so enormous, my feelings were so overwhelming, that it took my breath away. I wanted to do everything right, but I didn't know how.

I felt a bit overwhelmed and boxed in by my mother's hugs and tears, and later on by my father's. It was almost as if they wanted to squash me in their happiness. I had to relearn how to respond to spontaneous emotions devoid of any purpose or ulterior motive. Over the last several years the only protective "embrace" in a figurative sense had been my room underground. When I was down there alone, had enough to eat, and if I knew that the kidnapper would not come down for perhaps two or three days, because it was the weekend and his mother was upstairs. Those were the times where I could be myself, where I didn't have to be afraid and where I could feel safe.

It was during those times that I imagined the moment of our reunion quite often. Preferably somewhere in a distant galaxy or in a remote clearing, or on a boat with all the people who are important to me, but far, far out at sea, out of the reach of others. We would have enough to eat and drink on the boat, and would not come back to shore until we were ready.

In reality we were surrounded by strangers, by police officers and other people, and we were even strangers to each other, so that it couldn't be anything but awkward. Every look, gesture, question and answer was duly noted. Everybody expected us to be one happy family again at the touch of a button. And at that moment we were supposed to be this happy family simply due to the fact that a terrible period in our lives was now over. At the same time, we were simply not the kind of happy family you see in romantic Rosamunde Pilcher novels, where one occasion suffices to overcome the distances that have only become greater over the years. Of course it would have made for a wonderful headline: "Koch and Sirny fall into each other's arms, with their long-lost child in the middle. Will they finally get married now?" They had never been married, which was also a kind of black mark against us, "improper family circumstances", and the fact alone that we all had different names was repeatedly cause for confusion.

In a way we had stayed the same, with all of our positive and negative characteristics, the personal histories my parents carried with them, and with the new history that I had experienced and that cast everything in a dark shadow. A history whose dimensions my parents, the police officers surrounding us, and even I could not acknowledge at that moment. What had separated them over the last several years remained and could not be overcome. How could it have been any different, except at that one enormous moment when we first saw other again?

Too much had happened, particularly between the two of them. Anyone thinking back to the newspaper articles that were published during my abduction will still remember. My father had sought out the journalists who characterized my mother first as an "evil abusive mother" and later as a "potential murderess". He had called for investigations whenever detectives had announced that they now knew where I, or my bodily remains, were to be found, and even allowed himself to be filmed by a television crew, participating in a crime scene investigation with said detectives and a pond, which in the end was in fact drained. Of course without the desired result, but it achieved the desired ratings. Finally, my mother succeeded in taking legal action against just such baseless accusations.

My father was a willing victim of the media. Early on he adopted the role of the lonely and abandoned husband, who was continuing his investigation on his own, had had thousands of posters printed and hung up, while the rest of the family was apparently uninterested. Later in an interview I once said that he was very immature. Today I would no longer judge him so harshly, but rather characterize him as acting out of a certain naïveté, emphasizing that he was not always entirely fortunate in his choice of interview partners and in the wording of his statements. After my escape my attorneys received a rather sheepish telephone call from him on several occasions admitting, "I've really messed things up… Could you help me out?" He had told the media something in good faith, which was supposed to help me, as he saw it. But it resulted in headlines, such as "Koch casts doubt on daughter's statements and calls for further investigations. The entire truth must be finally uncovered".

During my captivity as well he certainly stumbled into many a mess, because he had always held tight to the conviction that I was still alive and that everything had to be done to find me after all. In his distress and hurt he had also given into the temptation to set himself up in opposition to my mother and to join the chorus singing that she was responsible for all of this.

My mother on the other hand had spoken to other media outlets who simply saw my father as an "idiot" with his fixation on ominous investigators and on her as the mastermind. He was painted as a chain-smoking drinker who never amounted to anything and was now looking to train the spotlight on himself as a result of what had happened to his daughter. The counterpunch usually came quite swiftly, often accusing my mother that she had made herself suspicious by not living up to the weeping, mourning stereotype. However, her life had been completely turned on its head, and nothing was as it used to be. No more proper family celebrations, no more Christmases the way they used to be, because one person was missing. My mother withdrew into her private world, losing herself in her work so as not to be reminded constantly of her loss. In the first several years she simply did not want to have anybody around. I am unable to express in words what the suspicions about her must have made her feel.

Perhaps I can put it this way: In an interview I once said something that I meant for my own situation at the time, but what could just as

74

easily have applied to hers. "At times I felt a bit like prey. Whenever it leaves its protective nest, it does not set out to become another animal's meal that day. It only becomes prey when it is hunted and torn apart by the pack of hunters. Only then does it become the victim, an object. And when the prey is injured during the hunt, it does not suddenly stop in midflight to lick its wounds. It only does so once it is once again in the safety of its burrow."

I made that statement at the time when I was being criticized for my supposed strength and the fact that I was never filmed or photographed crying. Is this what a traumatized victim looks like? Is this what a traumatized mother looks like?

My father dealt with his grief differently. He had no problem wearing his feelings on his sleeve. My mother, who kept a tight lid on her feelings, could not, or did not want to. Who can really play judge and jury about the right way to deal with such a loss? About who had suffered more or even had something to hide because they refused to break down before the eyes of the world.

With their very different ways of coping with my kidnapping, both of them provided amateur psychologists with plenty of fodder. In the end nobody can stand in judgment on what they really thought and felt during that time. On the extent to which they were in shock, and how that shock is still impacting their lives. Of course their suffering was different from what I went through. Still, we had to deal with the loss on both sides. My parents had to deal with the loss of their young daughter, without knowing whether or not she was still alive. And I had to deal with the loss of my freedom, in conjunction with the very high probability that I would never see my parents again, not to mention my elderly grandparents who at the time were already over seventy. One of the first questions that I asked my mother when I saw her again was whether my grandparents were still living. I was saddened when I found out that my favourite grandma, with whom I had always had a very special relationship, had already died two years prior to my escape.

My entire family is still suffering to this day from what happened. Even though they are once again living their lives and everything has returned to normal in a way. Each and every one of us – even my nieces and nephews – have suffered egregious harm. Of course I do not mean harm in the form of a serious personality disorder, but there is a sadness in them that won't go away. Their sadness is rooted in my kidnapping. This shadow continues to hang over all of us, which is largely due to the fact that the story keeps getting churned up again and again.

\*

I did not register any of this during my captivity. But all of this formed the backdrop for our first encounters after my escape.

In the car on the way to Vienna to the Criminal Police Office my mother bombarded the police officers with questions, such as "Does she have scars anywhere? Is she hurt? Will I even recognize her?"

We had no problems recognizing each other. But it took a while for us to realize how difficult it would be to truly bridge the gap that had been torn open over the last several years. We had no time and no peace and quiet to slowly get reacquainted. Even my reunion with my mother was splashed across the media, for example that I had said to her, "I know you didn't want all of this to turn out that way." For so many conspiracy theorists this was to be used as belated evidence that she had been working together with my kidnapper. However, I was only referring to our last morning together, when we parted ways still angry. Nobody can know just how much that scene weighed on my mother. That sentence fragment that she always tacked on to her comments when we were fighting – who knows when we'll see each other again – must have sounded like a dark prophecy.

She had missed her daughter for so long and would of course have loved to take me home with her more than anything else so that we could start up again where we had left off. The framed photographs that she sat in front of for hours with my grandmother and where she lit a candle on my birthday every year had been photographs of little Natascha. Now a different person was suddenly standing in front of her. It must be similar to when you return after many years and suddenly find only gigantic resort hotels where your idyllic beloved beach had once been.

We had not undergone the classic evolution like other mothers and daughters during puberty. No rituals, no pushing the relationship to another level. No behaviours that had evolved as well. Both of us only had our image of the other. Just like I was still the "little girl" for both of my sisters. My grandmother was the only one whose life was unaffected by this gap. Because the older generation had always adopted a different attitude and she had taken on a very special role in my life anyway.

In the first few weeks after my escape I was unsure as to how close direct contact with my family should be. I have already mentioned that the doctors had their own opinion on this. I needed distance from everything, and at the same time I did not want to offend anyone. Who, if not they, had never given up on me, even if the kidnapper had always told me differently. And still I was overwhelmed, having to adjust to a number of persons at once, all with different needs and interests, after having interacted with only one close person in my life for several years.

On 16 September 2006 I wrote in my diary:

*Family meeting!*
*It's about what my future is to be like. I have increasingly noticed that I am understandably still a stranger to my mother. There is this part of me that she has not yet accepted. She is vacillating back and forth helplessly between a lack of emotional detachment to the little girl I used to be, who she would like to put her arms around, and the daughter I am now. Essentially my feelings are the same. Only the other way around.*

I think that describes the situation we were in at the time rather well. We could not simply turn back the clock and pretend as if nothing had happened. While they hoped to cuddle and pamper me, I did not want to have freed myself from one dependency only to be subsumed by the next. I needed time until I was able to allow myself to be close to somebody again. Moreover, even as a child I had painted a very vivid picture in my mind of what it would be like to live my own life once I had reached the age of adulthood. This dream should be all the more understandable, considering that I had just now put years of absolute dominance by another behind me.

The fact that I preferred – for whatever reason – not to immediately move back into my old bedroom, but rather to move from the hospital to a nurses' residence and then to my own apartment were viewed very critically. The media made an issue out of whether we talked on the phone (yes, regularly even), how often we saw each other (how often do you see your parents?) and in what environment. Whether my father was present or not, and if not, why. Most articles adopted the stance that he was the only one who had gone stubbornly in search of the whole truth and continued to do so after my escape, which is why he was being punished with rejection by me and the rest of my family. The wedge between my parents, which had been fashioned even during my captivity, was now being driven down a bit deeper.

As the object of public scrutiny, we attempted to rebuild our lives as a family that had no longer existed even prior to my kidnapping. The answer to the question of whether I see my father, my mother, or my relatives and nieces and nephews every other day, every two weeks or every two years has nothing to do with my captivity.

Expectations were raised not only of me, but also of my parents, about how they were to act and how not. They too were forced to live up to an image – and failed to do so both in their own way. They had been people with their own personalities before the kidnapping; they had a prior history. You couldn't simply whitewash everything in an attempt to make everything okay again. And the corresponding conclusions were drawn from the fact that exactly this kind of outcome was not going to happen.

After my escape my father was treated by the press as an even greater laughingstock than in the years before. For example there was a cartoon depicting him as Scrooge McDuck jumping around between stacks of money and gold coins, telling me, "Great! You had only to be locked up in the cellar for eight and half years, and now we're laughing all the way to the bank!"

And when my mother wrote a book one year after my escape telling her story of the desperate years during my captivity, people wrote in letters and on the Internet: "Which one of you was worse off?" or "It's really dumb for your mother to whip off a book and beat you to the punch. Can't you forbid her at all from writing her book so you can still cash in all the way on your story? After all, that's what you're all about, isn't it?"

I most certainly had my problems with the book being published because, for example, my mother had written about things in her book that I had told her in confidence. For example, that I had said goodbye to the kidnapper at his coffin. I had once told him, "One day I will dance on your grave." Of course I did not do this, but I did feel a kind of satisfaction, a kind of victory in terms of "I survived this entire nightmare and you did not."

I did not want my visits to the morgue to be made public. Because it is difficult for those on the outside to put something like that in the right perspective. Because it's easier to write about the "strangely alienating grief" the victim is feeling for the kidnapper then about the complexity of the situation in which I had only one person I was close to for many, many years. On whom my survival depended, and with whom I had to find a way to come to terms. You can't just simply banish someone that you have spent eight and half years of your life with from your memory – no matter what the circumstances. I spent nearly as much of my life together with him as I had before the kidnapping with my family.

I tried to briefly outline our life together and my reaction to his death in my "letter to the world public", writing, "He carried me in his arms and trampled me underfoot. He was a part of my life. That is why I mourn for him in a way." By escaping I not only freed myself from my torturer, but also from a person who I had by necessity been close to.

Today I can understand a bit more easily that this was quite difficult to accept. Because the unyielding categories of good and evil would have to be reconsidered and the lines between them blurred. The kidnapper would have to be taken down from the height of monstrosity and inhumanity. He would have to regain a portion of his humanness. I have tried to do this over the years by seeing him as a person, with a very dark side, but also with a very light side. In so doing I have been able to remain human myself. I was able to, I had to forgive him for what he did to me, otherwise hate and anger would have eaten me up inside.

The public was unable to refrain from judging that attitude, and therefore my behaviour. It was seen instead as yet another piece of evidence that it couldn't have been as bad as all that. That I had perhaps even stayed with him willingly, because after all had there not been possibilities for escape earlier on?

All of that was continually reheated. After the presentation of the book I was asked what I thought about the fact that my mother was cashing in on "my story". I said at the time, "If she wants to tell her story to the public, then she should be allowed to do that. I would do things differently, but everybody has his or her own conscience and must consider what is ethically and morally acceptable and/or appropriate." It may have seemed harsh at first, and certainly my disappointment that a number of episodes from our new life together had been revealed played a part. Episodes that, in my view, did not belong in the public realm. Misunderstandings that prove how difficult we found it to understand each other's thoughts and actions. The story about the clothing, for example: she could not understand why I would want to keep some of the "rags" from my dungeon. Why I wouldn't throw them away or even better burn them, as if I could erase all of my horrible memories. During my captivity I found a great deal of comfort in certain items. I did not have very much to be happy about, and I had learned to recognize the greatness even in small things. The few T-shirts and socks that I had gave me warmth back then, and meant something positive to me.

And even if I viewed a number of things with a critical eye – so much had been building up in my mother for so many years and had to be released. And it was her decision to do it the way she did. The risk that entailed was something both of us had to cope with in equal measure.

Portions of her book became the focus of further articles and blogs aimed at defamation and exposure. The press speculated as to whether my father would take legal action against the book, because he was not depicted very favourably. There were rumours about a final split between my parents and me, as well as about a tearful reconciliation. Black or white, there do not seem to be very many shades of nuance in between.

In the first three years after my escape we regularly met at a farm near the village of Mariazell to celebrate life together. We needed time to get to know each other again, to become more natural with each other, also in dealing with how we were being portrayed.

In the meantime we have found a very good level for our relationship. I bake and sew with my mother regularly. We often go shopping together or out to eat, or do something with my sisters and their children. The waters have calmed between my father and me as well.

We likely would have been able to bridge the distance between us faster if there had been less scorched earth remaining after the commentators, bloggers, analysts and caricaturists had set aside their pens or their keyboards.

4

# *"Just Go out Dancing!"*

## *My Struggle for Normalcy*

Everybody was telling me now that I had to go out to a club, to meet young people, as if that would be the solution to all my problems. Of course that wouldn't work, because it was a bit like "playing teenager". Hitchhiking through the countryside with a blade of grass between my teeth and doing other things that young people do.

After my short intermezzo in the nurses' residence I moved to my mother's flat temporarily until I could find a flat of my own. I did not have a great many ideas about what I wanted, and I had very few requirements. I wanted it to be full of light, have as few walls as possible, a great deal of glass, under no circumstances in the basement, but rather somewhere high above the ground, a room with a view so to speak.

After my conscious decision to eschew my status as a "patient guinea pig", the team of those people who were now to officially accompany me down my new path had suddenly become much smaller. Those who were still part of the team - my attorneys and a social worker - were now faced with the thankless task of searching for an apartment for an anonymous person. Of course the landlord later found out who was to move in, but we didn't want to advertise that it was me from the very beginning. The apartment had to be affordable in the long run, because nobody knew if and when I would be able to stand on my own two feet financially, if I would ever be able to have a profession, or what the future held in general. Because I had been kidnapped on my way to school, I received a small annuity. And the Austrian Broadcasting Corporation (ORF) had, as previously mentioned, set up an account after my interview to receive the money from the international sales of the broadcasting rights and private donations. But I did not want to touch that money for my flat, because I wanted to use it to help others. The original plan of setting up a foundation could not be implemented unfortunately, as we fell short of the amount needed for the initial deposit. All the money was left in the bank until I could find a suitable use for it.

On the day of my escape my personal "wealth" amounted to € 416. The kidnapper gave me an allowance of 10 Austrian schillings a week, which he later generously rounded up to € 1. At the time I thought it a rather ridiculous, helpless attempt to establish normalcy between an adult and a child, even though nothing was normal and there was no way I could buy any kind of sweets with my money just like other kids. Over the years I saved it in the same plastic box that I kept my passport in.

Aside from the few items of clothing from the dungeon, I owned nothing. From my toothbrush to cosmetics to a skirt or a coat to wear, I needed to buy everything new. I asked everybody around me what toothpaste they used. In the drugstore I examined all of the packages 1,000 times, reading every word of the list of ingredients. Sometimes it took hours for me to make a decision. Every item of clothing was examined from top to bottom, evaluated according to its quality and usefulness, and then found to be too expensive. I had no sense of how much things cost, and I preferred to put it back on the rack before I made a mistake. As a girl I most often wore what my mother had sewn for me or had purchased in a boutique, because she liked to outfit me with pretty clothes. And later I only had the very few items of clothing the kidnapper had brought me anyway.

I had absolutely no idea where the best place to buy a winter coat was, and in a few months I was certain to need one. I was completely overwhelmed by the many shops in the pedestrian area with their overflowing display windows. I also did not like trying things on in the dressing room, where it was all too clear in the large mirror and under the harsh lighting how much my captivity had affected me physically. Stepping out from behind the curtain, I was eyed with curiosity by the sales staff. Other shoppers stopped to whisper, "Hey, that's Natascha Kampusch!" Some people pulled out their mobiles and took pictures of me, wanted an autograph or told one of the many jokes about me making the rounds in a loud and clear voice while walking past, like one comparing me to a used car that had been primarily kept in the garage the whole time. Startled, I jumped back behind the curtain.

Also because I didn't want to subject myself to situations like those any longer, I had learned to sew my own clothes in the meantime myself. My mother taught me the basics, how to place a pattern on the material, how much leeway to leave, what kind of stitches to make, etc. We were able to overcome the distance that had arisen due to our long separation best by sewing together or thumbing through sewing magazines. She was the master seamstress, and I was her student. However, there was more friction between us when we were cooking. Here I was still a child to her, for whom she had once made sandwiches for school, or lunch or dinner. I still remembered a "baking demonstration" at the hospital quite well. It was my nephew's birthday, and I was bound and determined to bake a cake. There was a small staff kitchen in the hospital that I was allowed to use. I asked my mother to gather up the ingredients and bring them to the hospital. I had planned to make the cake crust out of choux pastry and fill it with different kinds of fruit and gelatine. A number of nurses and my mother hovered over me, asking where my recipe was. After all you have to stick to the exact weight measurements when baking, otherwise it won't turn out right, they would say. Why aren't you making a crust out of sponge cake or a regular cake mixture? Where did you learn to bake in the first place?

I thought to myself, they should just wait and see. As calmly as possible I mixed the water in the milk together with butter and a bit of sugar in a pot that I then placed on the stove. After bringing the mixture to a bubble, I mixed in the flour. One of the nurses said that she had never before seen cake batter cooked on the stove. Before I put it in the oven, I added the eggs, then I began making the filling. I mixed the canned fruit together, warmed it on the stove and added the gelatine. "Come on Natascha. You have to do it this way; otherwise it'll get all lumpy." It wasn't until I told her to please wait, that I knew what I was doing, that she held her tongue. But her sceptical looks continued. When the choux pastry dough was finished, I let it cool for just a few minutes before adding the thickened fruit mixture.

There were certainly room for improvement in my visual presentation, but it was my first cake baked in freedom, and that is why it tasted particularly good not just to me, but also to the birthday boy. Even my mother, who is always particularly critical, had words of praise. It seemed that I had indeed absorbed considerable know-how from my family's history as bakers, she said.

Ever since then I have baked numerous cakes, and aside from one unsuccessful experiment with the natural sweetener Stevia, there have never been any complaints. I am sometimes teased by my friends for my domestic abilities. When I spend days baking cookies at Christmas, they say, "You're just like my grandma." And just like "grandma" I know a lot of home remedies for removing stains or for dying cloth using natural ingredients. That may seem a bit out of step with the times, but that's how I feel myself from time to time. Neither young nor old, I am somehow caught between ages.

I particularly like handicrafts, because it calms me and I can let my creativity run wild. I have even designed accessories such as jewellery or handbags myself. I had already begun to do so while in captivity. With crochet yarn that I had requested for Christmas from the kidnapper. I still have a number of those small bags that I crocheted at the time.

Even as a child handicrafts and painting were my way of withdrawing into my own little world whenever I felt unable to find my place in the world outside. In the dungeon, I needed pictures, pictures from my world even from my old world that I could use to counter my present reality. I coloured the tongue-and-groove boards that covered the walls of my dungeon in the beginning, before they were replaced by drywall panels, with crayons. I drew a door handle on the door, just like the one in my mother's apartment. And next to it a small dresser that stood in the hallway. When I lay on my bed and closed my eyes, I would imagine that the door would open at any moment. My mother would come in and put her keys on the dresser. I drew my family tree, the silver Mercedes on the wooden boards, horses in a meadow with flowers. An illusion, nothing more. But when I stared intensely enough at the images, I had the feeling that I could almost smell the flowers.

Even today pictures are very important to me. I paint with acrylic, tempera or oil paints, and I enjoy photography. After one of my first interviews I was given a small digital camera that I used to capture this new colourful world. I was fascinated by details and other trivialities that many perhaps do not find worthy of being photographed. Things that people take for granted in their everyday lives, for example two glasses on the table bathed in a ray of sunlight. In the meantime the camera has become a tool for me to create distance. To filter the many impressions raining down on me, or focus them on one point or moment, to transform something into an object and not to become an object myself.

\*

In my first interview with Christoph Feurstein he asked me what my very first wish was that I had fulfilled after my escape. That was the only question that threw me for a loop a little bit. I glanced over to my team of advisors and ask them, "Can anyone remember?" After a few moments I answered, "The main wish that I fulfilled for myself in the last several days is naturally freedom. (…) mmm, yes, and I went to get some ice cream in disguise. On Währingerstrasse in an ice cream parlour." Wearing a scarf on my head and sunglasses.

Going for ice cream. How often had I imagined doing just that during my captivity. A spoonful of ice cream, first cold and firm, slowly melting, until the taste of hazelnut or vanilla or strawberry filled your entire mouth. That was also a game with illusions. Using advertising brochures that I thumbed through, I would embark on similar adventures of taste. I would look for an appetizer, a main course and a dessert. For hours on end. Despite how unable I was to fill my empty stomach with those pictures, going for ice cream in freedom made up for it somewhat.

I was thankful for now having the opportunity to eat ice cream whenever I wanted to. But no matter how many scoops of ice cream I ate, it would always taste different from the ice cream that you enjoy while sitting with friends in an ice cream parlour laughing, complaining about an annoying teacher or gushing about your latest crush. In the beginning whenever I would see a happy clique of young people somewhere, I felt a stab of envy. I wondered if I would be able to enjoy something similar someday. How did you define friendship in the first place? I still had to find that out for myself. My last memories of friendship were from my childhood, although I was more an outsider and not the class clown at the centre of attention. I was only the centre of attention when my father came to school during recess with a box full of fresh jelly donuts from the bakery. Teachers often found me somewhat unpleasant, because I was very direct and spoke up when I sensed an injustice or an untruth some-where. I simply wanted to be authentic, but I simply did not notice that I was hurting other people's feelings. There were many situations where I was admonished or punished by adults for that very reason, which I could not understand at all. "Just look at what you've done again!" I got the impression that it is apparently easier sometimes to maintain a lie or to sugarcoat something than to face up to the truth. As if you had to sprinkle cinnamon on it in order to make it more palatable.

With my openness, there were phases after my escape where I kept putting my foot in my mouth. Depending on his or her degree of social-ization, everybody from a certain age onward is no longer very malleable, and certain basic character traits have long been established. Before my kidnapping I already had a personality, history that was longer than the time I had spent in captivity. Children see the world with open eyes. They know more than grown-ups give them credit for, because they use their intuition for many things that grown-ups try to comprehend with their minds.

In captivity it helped that a portion of my personality had already been so well-established that I could uphold a value system that I felt was right for me. In many areas I was in opposition to the kidnapper. Not on principle, as is sometimes the case in puberty when teenagers try to distance themselves from their parents, although their views are perhaps not all that worthy of rebellion. People mount the barricades in order to carve out their place in the world, to liberate themselves from actual or supposed constraints. People try things out, push the envelope and feel free while doing it.

I stood in opposition to the kidnapper simply due to the fact that everything about what he had done was wrong. When he said "blue", I thought to myself "red". When he got worked up over a political event, about all the incompetents who in the good old days, under Adolf, would have gone nowhere fast, when law and order prevailed, I would think to myself "anarchy!" And when he held forth about his conservative stance on women – she should be industrious, wait for him at home with dinner, not contradict, always be nice and neat – and when he would say to me, "I am your king. You must serve me," I would try to carry out my chores as slowly or as sloppily as possible, even if I was punished for it. These attempts to distance myself from him were other victories than the ones that others my age achieved when they defied their parents' wishes.

In captivity I could only see everything in relation to myself. Aside from the kidnapper, there was no one else. He was the only one I had to adapt to, the only one I had to accommodate. Over time I learned to read his behaviour. I knew that not only was I dependent on him, but to a certain degree he was dependent on me as well. In his split personality, for example, he could not bear it if I remain silent or punished him with my contempt. While renovating once I handed him the wrong tool. From one second to the next the look in his eyes turned insane. Everything about him was pure rage. I had never seen him like that before. He grabbed a sack of cement and threw it at me full force, making me lose my balance for a moment. Everything hurt, and tears sprang to my eyes. But I would not allow him that triumph I remained standing as stiff as a board, only staring at him. "Come on. Stop it now. I'm sorry. It wasn't really that bad." He came over to me, shook my shoulders, pinched my side and used his fingers to push the corners of my mouth upward. "Come on, laugh a bit. I'm sorry. Please go back to normal again. What can I do to make you normal again?"

It wasn't until an eternity had passed that I moved and said, "I want ice cream and gummy bears." Childish pragmatism and the attempt to downplay the seriousness of the attack with my demand. At times Priklopil would have given an obstinate three-year-old a run for his money. First break the toy and then despair that it is broken. But of course it makes a difference whether a three-year-old child is kicking you and yelling at you and is angry at you and destroys everything, or whether it is a strong, 1.72 metre tall man.

*

In my letter to the "world public" as previously mentioned, I wrote that the kidnapper carried me in his arms and trampled me underfoot. A half a year after my escape an article was published in the newspaper referring to me as the "queen from the cellar dungeon". It described me as a strange creature, an extremely empathetic woman, but also one with regal airs and graces. "Her apparently limitless empathy is understandable: She truly knows how much a person can suffer. But her regal bearing is also easily explained: after all, during her captivity she was the centre of all attention. An enormous effort was made exclusively for her in order to assure her captivity. And her fortune was that she knew that in that construct she was the dominant one, and not the man who thought that he had snatched a toy off the street. She was unable to expand her limited knowledge of social behaviour, as she was only able to learn absolute domination, albeit ex negativo. And it was this domination that kept her from being paraded about later on."[*]

Even though I would definitely not attribute a "regal attitude" to myself, one thing was certainly correct: everything the kidnapper did was focused on me. The beatings as well as the gummy bears. I was able to read his responses – as long as they were not completely irrational and did not come from out of the blue – whether he saw my behaviour as right or wrong.

After my escape I had difficulty at first switching off this mechanism. I observed people, trying to interpret their facial expressions and to figure out how they were meant in relation to myself. If a waiter at a restaurant was unfriendly, I first looked to myself to figure out why, never thinking that he perhaps had simply gotten up on the wrong side of

---

[*] http://www.welt.de/vermischtes/article704105/Die-Koenigin-aus-dem-Kellerverlies.html (Version: August 2016)

the bed that day, or simply was generally a grouchy person. I didn't dare go shopping alone, because I was sure that everybody could tell how lost I felt. People simply staring off into space in my direction in the Vienna metro made me feel like Big Brother was watching me.

I had to learn that it was not always about me and to take things more in stride. And just when I was making considerable headway in navigating public spaces more confidently and light-heartedly, the setbacks came. With supposedly new revelations, the reopening of the case, with corresponding comments in the media. There was no other choice than to understand that the reactions rebounding on me were, in fact, all about me. Nobody else was there to absorb the blows.

*

Regaining my confidence was a process that took a long time. Whenever I met somebody for the first time, it was very rarely in a very neutral, unbiased way. At a party, other people were able to talk about their lives completely normally, a little story here, a brief anecdote there. At first I thought I was lacking in something that I was unable to contribute anything, aside from my very particular life story. I had no shared memories with girlfriends, no holidays with my parents. I only had memories that were connected to the kidnapper. The responses to my stories always shifted from one extreme to the other: "Please stop it right now. I don't want to hear anything like that." Even if I was just talking about a harmless scene in a drugstore, and I casually mentioned, "Oh, I had that mint toothpaste too. I didn't like it at all." Or my unique life story was all we talked about, and nothing else.

I am happy that I have been able to construct a new story somewhat in the last ten years. I have made some friends who do not only see me as the kidnapper's creation or the product of my years in captivity, but rather tried to accept me with all of my contradictions. They tried to see me as a whole person. Some of them are already somewhat older and can look back on their own personal stories replete with ups and downs. Maybe that's why they are able to be so easy going with me. Mostly at first, I got the feeling from people my own age that there was an enormous gulf separating us. I missed out on an entire phase of my life that can simply never be recovered. I have honestly tried to go out into the world, surround myself with young people and have fun, also because many people advised me to. I have been to clubs because I like music and I like to dance, but I have to admit that I don't get much out of it. Add to that the smoke, and the stuffy air, and the confined space. It's hard to be relaxed and carefree at the touch of a button. And that has been ultimately impossible ever since I have become a person of public interest in the wake of my kidnapping.

I still vividly remember one evening when I went to a club called "Wiener Passage" with a number of young employees from my attorneys' law offices. We danced and talked, and when I wanted to leave after a while, one of the young men hugged me and gave me a goodbye kiss on my cheek. It just so happened that a party photographer was on hand at the club who snapped a picture at just the right moment.

I was irritated, but basically it was a harmless affair. We knew each other. What did it matter? However, the next morning I got a call from a well-known daily newspaper. The person on the other end of the line said that she had pictures with "compromising" images in front of her on the desk. I didn't entirely understand what she was getting at and said that I didn't recall having been in a compromising situation in the past several days. She explained a bit further, only to reassure me immediately that she would do everything in her power to make sure that the pictures were not published. I only needed to agree to an exclusive interview. I did not want to allow myself to be blackmailed, so I rejected her offer. It seems that the editorial desk got cold feet. In the meantime my attorneys had succeeded in obtaining temporary injunctions. The pictures were not published in that newspaper, but surfaced a couple days later in another gossip rag: "Her first love is sooo sweet – Natascha Kampusch has a boyfriend." A "cool youngster" with "Hugh Grant hair", who let the waistband of his dark blue briefs peek out of the top of his pants."

On a side note, that evening also served as a jumping off point for critical think pieces and comments about what someone like me was even doing in the club after eight and half years of captivity. It was reprehensible and evidence of my licentiousness and lack of morals.

On another occasion I was invited to the after-show party after the final of "Starmania", Austria's version of "Pop Idol". Hundreds of people were at the ORF television studios at Künigelberg. I was having difficulty with all of the confusion and trying to make small talk with people I didn't know. I was tired and weary from the sensory overload, and sat down at a table for a moment by myself. In front of me was a plate with leftover food and a number of empty bottles and glasses with dregs of alcohol in the bottom. The headline the next day: "Natascha Kampusch – Too Much to Drink? Has her past broken her?"

I don't drink alcohol, and I'm not the type to go clubbing or out to bars all night. But even if I were, why should anybody care? During my lost childhood I would have loved to have the choice to go out and enjoy life, no matter where or how. And now when people are telling me to open up, discover the world, I was not allowed to do just that, because it was immoral, or because the press would impute some kind of affair or problem to me.

The worst part was that people who were supporting me and actually wanted to protect me ended up being pulled into the public spotlight themselves. How could I have seriously made any friends under these circumstances? Even today people who are closest to me do not want to go out into the city with me. Because they have been accosted regularly in restaurants or coffee houses as soon as I had gone to the toilet, and because they have been photographed and stared at. Only being able to meet in one's own home in order to be left in peace is a limitation that I have found extremely irritating many times.

In the meantime I have come to enjoy cooking for friends at home, eating together and spending a couple of agreeable hours sitting around the table much more. But it's different if you do that because that's what you want, because you have decided that it's more to your liking then bar-hopping with a large group friends, where it's difficult to engage in more in-depth conversation. Or whether you have the feeling that you have no choice. I'm happy that in the meantime I have been able to find out for myself what I prefer and what I don't. It is really just a coincidence that what began as a gradual withdrawal from public spaces is exactly what I needed. For a long time I tried to do what other people were so convinced would help me. I thought that they would be the ones to know, as they had enough life experience after all. They had grown up in freedom, and I hadn't. It took a while for me to even pinpoint my needs and interests once again. In the meantime I have established what I like and I can set my own boundaries.

\*

The only thing that I definitely was able to articulate about what I wanted after my escape was that I wanted to complete my education.

Around the end of 2006, in the beginning of 2007 I began my studies to complete my compulsory schooling. I earmarked three years to achieve my goal. One reason was because I was unable to judge what would be on the exams. I fluctuated between "You can do it" and self-doubt. Aside from a couple years of elementary school, the only foundation that I had was what I had acquired during captivity. Knowledge from encyclopaedias and books. I enjoyed reading texts about altitudes, the length of rivers, their water levels, anything geographical really. I also liked statistics and numbers. I think numbers are beautiful. There's something honest about them. They cannot be misused the same way words can.

The kidnapper as well would teach me things from time to time using the old school books he had kept. His motivation was certainly the fact that, as he once said, he "couldn't stand stupid people", so it was in his interest for me to develop my mind. However, the same time he used studying with me as a tool to exercise power and dominance. He was particularly gleeful to take a red pencil to my exercises. In my German essays, the subject matter was secondary, with the main focus on correct grammar and spelling. Rules, rules, rules. They had to be followed at all costs. Whenever I made the same mistake several times in different "classroom periods", he would scold and punish me. "You are too stupid to shit" or "You're doing that on purpose just to irritate me". The punishment dependent on his mood. Most of the time he knew exactly how to hurt me most at any given moment. If he saw a book lying open on my bed, he would turn the light off for the rest of the day. If I had casually told him about a cassette with an interesting audio play, he would take the batteries out of my Walkman. And if I asked him for a glass of water before study time, because I was terribly thirsty, I would most certainly have to go without a drink until the next day.

On the other hand I was so hungry for an education that I wanted to tackle the new material in order to absorb all this new information. In addition, I wasn't used to concentrating on one subject over a longer period of time, to working in a very mentally structured way. I wanted to do much too much, and all of it at once, and most of all down to the last detail. I wanted to be free to contemplate everything in peace, and also to think outside the box from time to time, in order to recognize interconnections and to avoid just "working the program". I did not want to consume education, I wanted to grasp it.

The Vienna School Board thankfully made it possible for me to complete my compulsory schooling at a co-operative middle school. In the afternoon, I was given individual instruction by a team of teachers in various subjects. Due to my age and my particular situation, the idea of joining the other children in class was quickly discarded. The idea was not only to protect me but also the other students, whose everyday schooling was not to be disrupted. In the beginning I was a bit disappointed at this. I would've liked to have experienced what it's like to be integrated into a normal school system. But looking back, it was probably the right decision, because after all my years of being alone, I am used to working at my own pace and learning on my own.

I was happy that I had finally passed my exams. I had fewer problems with the material than I had feared. However, I proved to be an obstacle to myself at times, because I was very strict with myself. That is certainly a result of my captivity, where I was never able to do anything right, never praised, but only shown all the things I couldn't do or did wrong.

With my diploma in hand I wanted to tackle the next step, namely passing the "Matura", the secondary school leaving exam in Austria. The fact that I already begun had come up in an interview. I would have preferred to keep it my little secret. As a result, this put more pressure on me, because people kept asking how far along I had come. I was happy that people were taking an interest, but at the same time their questions made me uncomfortable. I felt like a lazy student, trapped between my own perfectionism and an overly cautious approach. Only when I am sure that I have mastered something do I dare take the next step. I would rather look over my work once again before handing in a hastily scribbled essay or where I'm sure that I failed to completely follow all of the proper steps to get the right answer. This can be easily misinterpreted as insecurity or incompetence, but in fact it is simply a slow preparation process, a comprehensive approach in the hope of achieving a better result.

To make matters worse, my preparations for the Matura came at a time where I was very much the focus of public scrutiny, because the "Kampusch case" was being reopened again. With the determined result being the fact that I had told the truth, that Priklopil had acted alone,

and, and, and. Hardly had the established result reached the public domain, once again somebody immediately began doubting it; the ma-
chinery of the judicial system, committees, press reports ... once again
sprang into action.

I had to appear in court on numerous occasions and was questioned
on particular events again and again: whether the kidnapper had done
this or that, whether I knew his mother or not, what the situation in the
house and in the dungeon was like, why I had written this or another
entry in my diary, or if I knew what I did on a particular date in year X.
All of the statements were then compared to the police reports drawn up
during my initial questioning. They were no deviations that could have
provided all of those "seekers of the real truth" any ammunition. Nevertheless, the permanent feedback loop continued, and it dealt me a massive setback during that phase of my life. Because all of the old wounds
were reopened, because I was forced to return to a time that I had found
a different way of coping with in the meantime – also thanks to therapy.
My captivity had moved somewhat farther into the distant past. And I
was trying to get my new life under control. And yet I was forced again
and again to revisit it. To allow that time back into my life, and more
than was already the case. The past, or what we experience in life, will always be a part of us. Sometimes its presence will be foregrounded more,
sometimes less, but most of the time without directly impacting our
present. Over time and with the help of therapy I have learned to deal
with memories and flashbacks so that they do not permanently weigh on
me, hurt me or erect an insurmountable wall between me and the rest
of my life.

And now I had crashed against a wall that was constantly being
rebuilt from the outside. I would never have opposed any further investigations if the focus were genuinely on new findings. I never even
opposed this theatre of the absurd that was now being staged. I was available, provided statements, even when it was no longer about confirming
facts or clarifying questions by a long shot. My past was the backdrop,

or the chessboard on which many a figure advanced and retreated. My presence, my struggle to find normalcy was unimportant.

It was in exactly this atmosphere that I was attempting to pass the Matura. And whenever I was repeatedly asked whether I already had my Matura in hand and was thinking about tackling university studies soon, I sometimes felt like a juggler attempting to juggle five balls in public for the first time. Everything went so smoothly at home, but now he can't help but drop all the balls at once. And even if I knew that I had not really dropped all of the balls, for the audience or the reader it must have sounded like I had failed. Because I kept saying that I was still working on it.

In fact I was paralyzed for a time due to all of the turbulence. All of the upset and stress caused me to fear taking the exam. In the meantime I have successfully passed the first portions of the exam, in art among other subjects. The rest will follow in time. I am grateful that I now have so many options open to me, that I can take a number of avenues to develop myself further. The journey is the most important thing for me. Life leads you to so many forks in the road, and I wanted to have the freedom to change my mind whenever I wanted about which path to take. If it's to be university studies, great. If not, that's fine too. I may be seen as too fickle or lacking in direction in our rather achievement-oriented society. But I see that a bit differently. Just recently I said to a friend that I sometimes wished for a life-sized third knitting needle, like the one you use when you set some of the stitches aside for later. Until you have figured out how to continue the pattern.

5

# *Stopped Short*

## *My Difficult Search for a Purpose*

It is perhaps unusual that someone like me can develop an entrepreneurial spirit so quickly, put her nose to the grindstone and want to make an impact. Many people simply didn't understand, but that's just the way I am. I thought I would jump into life with both feet. Someone else may have withdrawn to the safety of their family, cried a lot. But not everybody is the same, but every approach to working through your experiences in life should be seen as legitimate. Essentially, people should really be happy that I am now doing something worthwhile.

However, it took me a while to come to this realization; all too often I allowed myself to be distracted from living my life by influences from the outside. Sometimes even those close to me were overwhelmed in sorting through my many ideas and pointing them in a direction that either made sense to them or was merely feasible. Once we had a heated discussion where I was constantly being told, this was not possible, because... Charity work yes, but only together with "the right institutions"; I was "taboo" for work in other areas. But that was not what I wanted. I was already being asked for my "expertise as a victim" on a regular basis, any time a case of abuse or an egregious crime was uncovered that was comparable to the one perpetrated against me. But comparisons are not possible, because every case is different, every victim is different, and every criminal is different. I do not want to assume that I can make a judgment as someone on the outside looking in.

Moreover, I did not want to shore up my status as a victim, but I wanted to convey other messages if I was to be addressing the public anyway. Like having courage, being a role model for others and that you can regain control over your life. That you can turn the suffering that you experienced into something positive. I would have liked to talk about the "strategies" that have helped me to survive. Here as well it is important to keep in mind that everyone is different, but perhaps some of my advice could have been helpful to someone. Contributions like these are very rarely asked for; most of the time the focus was on the suffering that I had experienced. Even when the topic was my future, it could not be separated from my past. It was like it ran on automatic, as if I had to compete with myself in my attempt to reinvent a "new" Natascha as an improvement on the "old" one.

*

The statement I heard most often in the discussions about my future was, "You can't do that, because you're too famous." Almost as a joke I once said, great, then I can apply for a job in television, because fame is, after all, not an obstacle.

For a moment everybody looked at each other astonished. Maybe that really was an option? Of course I had no experience in that field, other than having played news anchor as a child, or pretended to host television shows for adopting homeless pets, sitting in front of the mirror on the rattan chair, with my mother's cats in my lap. In the dungeon I staged my own television shows, playing scenes from series, such as Alf, Married with Children or Star Trek. The science fiction shows fascinated me most of all. The heroes and heroines in the stories travelled to far-off galaxies and were able to use a holodeck to create virtual worlds, not just in their heads, but worlds that they could actually move around in. In my imagination I journeyed to innumerable worlds. And how I would've liked to possess the technical means to beam myself away from life-threatening situations.

Later on I was a regular listener to the talk show Im Gespräch with Peter Huemer on the radio. It was fascinating for me to listen to him and his guests and follow their thought processes and articulated ideas. In fact, I actually found radio better than television, because nothing is there to distract you from what is being said. No colourful stage back-drop, no moderators playing to the cameras so that the TV audience does not change the channel. It is somehow honest and more focused on the actual subject matter.

I really couldn't imagine myself on TV. It was a crazy idea, but at the same time an opportunity to turn the tables. I wasn't the one to answer the questions, but rather to ask them. And I would ask questions that not only I found interesting, but hopefully my TV audience as well. I could interview interesting people within the framework of a new for-mat, and perhaps also offer "normal" people, not only celebrities, with an unusual life story a platform.

I am in essence somebody who is interested in other people. I have an extremely acute talent for observation, and I'm able to react quickly and adapt to a changing situation. I perfected all of these skills while in captivity. But would it be enough? There were a number of heavily qualified journalists who would be quite happy to moderate a talk show. Wjhy would anybody decide to let me have a go?

I knew that it would be fun for me. In Barcelona, exactly one year after my escape, I had slipped into the role of questioner for the first time. The editorial team from the television show Thema had accompanied my sister and me for a few days on my first trip outside Austria after my captivity. They were looking for a different angle, not a studio interview with boilerplate questions like: "How are you doing now, one year later?" They were looking for something new, something that was to portray me from a more comprehensive angle. Not just in a serious one-on-one dialogue, but also carefree, strolling around the city or on the beach. I had willingly agreed to participate because it was my feeling that I owed it to the many people who had shared their honest empathy with me to give them an update on how far I had come.

Most likely the Scottish Highlands or somewhere in Scandinavia would have been better for my sensitive skin, but I had a number of romantic ideas about what Barcelona was like. The very particular teardrop architectural style of Gaudí that reminded me of the sand structures that my schoolmates had built over the summer holidays, with photographs of them passed around for everybody to admire. Colourful sun lounges on the beach, sunshades, and in the background the blue sea. Up until then I had never been to the ocean. I knew a little bit about Spain from television. More like clichés of busy streets, where sooner or later somebody always dances a Flamenco, accompanied by someone singing. Impressive buildings reminiscent of glorious centuries gone by, and of course bullfighting. For me as a vegetarian and died in the wool animal activist that seemed to me to be rather dubious entertainment...

In the airplane I poured over the city map and the tourist guide book. We had a very full itinerary (including an evening of Flamenco!), and I did not want to be just trotting along behind the tour guide, letting her words wash over me. I wanted to be prepared. When we got there, the city was very different than I had expected. It was boiling hot, deafeningly loud and a thick cloud of smog hung over the city, making it difficult to breathe. Our hotel was close to the pedestrian mall La Rambla, but turned out to be under construction. The lobby was lost in plastic sheeting, and torn open bags of cement lying on the ground. Workers were drilling and hammering, making it difficult to hear oneself even think. Then, once in the room belonging to the ORF television crew, they opened the door to the closet and a bunch of junk fell out. After discussion about what to do, we decided to change hotels.

The new hotel was located at the old port, where only cruise ships now docked. Enormous luxury boats spitting out tourists from all over the world. Just like us, they poured through the narrow streets, fanned out to ride the double-decker buses taking them to see the most famous sights. I was only able to see Gaudí's Sagrada Família church from the outside, because the wait to get in would have made too big a dent in our itinerary. After a tour of the city, we went up to the Park Güell, up innumerable steps and stairs, aligned by beautiful oleander bushes, palm trees, agave plants and other exotic vegetation. The noise of the city was reduced to a soft buzzing in the background. Colourful parrots squawked, and the blossoms attracted swarms of buzzing bees and other insects.

Here as well we were not the only tourists with camera in hand, but the masses of people were more sparsely distributed across the entire area of the park measuring approximately 17 hectares than in the city down below. Only in front of Gaudí's former residence, now housing a museum, had a long line formed. We strolled through the park. I was fascinated by the buildings with their conspicuous "icing topped" roofs and the large terrace surrounded by an oval wall. You can sit on the wall, whose entire surface is decorated with the smallest ceramic and crystal tiles. The mosaics form a collage depicting abstract and figurative elements, such as flowers, fish or stars. I could've wandered around there for hours absorbing all of the painstakingly crafted details. Even if it sounds cheesy: art sometimes moves me to tears. It doesn't have to be made by human hands. The art that is hidden in nature sometimes exhibits a much more powerful, aesthetic attraction. At home I have an entire collection of small works of art from nature. Shells and stones that I get out from time to time, photograph, or touch. They have a lot to say about how the earth and life came about, and represent a link to the ages for me.

The next day we drove just a few minutes out of the city heading for the beach. Amazingly, there were very few people there. The section where we were did not even have those endless rows of sun loungers that I had seen in the holiday photos of my elementary school friends. The water was wonderful, and after a few minutes I had forgotten that a camera was filming me. I could have floated there forever. A voice brought me back to the present saying, "The sun is going to go down soon. And we still want to do the interview!"

Right at the beginning of the interview the focus was on the issue of trust. Whether I was able to be more open when interacting with others, and how I was able to deal with all of the impressions bombarding me from the outside world. I am unable, even today, to be fully and completely trustful. And it took actually three years for me to be able to handle the visual, acoustic and olfactory stimuli. Whenever I was sitting in the car or on the train, I would get dizzy from watching the landscape whiz by. I was unable to sift through the images so quickly, and the same applied to voices in a group of people. I always heard and perceived everything all at once, and if I was unable to identify a sound, my heart would begin to hammer. At the beginning I asked myself why other people had no problems doing so. Why did they not suffer from sensory overload? How do they cope when everything is layered on top of everything else, from perfume to aftershave, not to mention the odour of food or automobile exhaust? Did they lack sensitivity, or were there sensors poorly adjusted? No, they had simply gotten used to it. It has only been over the years that I have learned that life is much easier when you can rid yourself of the kind of hyper sensitivity that I had developed in captivity.

One year after my escape I was still having difficulty talking about the past and the present, which at the time were still rather interwoven, more than they are today. In the middle of the interview I asked Christoph Feurstein to turn off the camera, because I still had saltwater in my eyes. He understood my ulterior motive perfectly, and after a short break he suggested that we film each other for the interview. Just like when I take photographs, the small handheld video camera helped me to put a bit more distance between me and my situation and the subject matter of our interview once again.

For the rest of the interview we increasingly switched roles. And questions asked by me soon led to a back-and-forth, where the topic was not just on how I was processing my personal history, but rather the fundamental questions of life that we all wrestle with. For me at the time Barcelona stirred up quite a bit once again, but also put a great deal back in its proper place. I wanted to gain control of my life and do something with it.

\*

What began as a definite idea was announced several months later as a "media coup". After a couple of initial exploratory meetings and a number of camera tests, the decision was made to give me my own talk show on the channel Puls 4 in 2008. The channel had been taken over by the media group SevenOne in 2007. Its programming platform was to be completely redesigned, and new ideas developed. The plan was to produce six episodes of a 45 minute format, each with one guest who was to answer in-depth questions, without any sensationalistic, tell-all ulterior motives and without violating the privacy of my interview partner.

In the run-up there was a long discussion about how to conduct an interview and techniques for asking questions, which included Peter

Huemer and Georg Danzer's son.* This turned into an hours-long con-versation, at the end of which both gentlemen encouraged me to give it a try. A pilot phase lasting several months was to launch the project, where my first interviews with interesting people were recorded. I was to receive elocution lessons and learn how to remain calm and relaxed in the very unique studio atmosphere.

The reactions from my friends and family were divided. The fact that I was already suffering from my fame, that it was such an enormous burden on me, was an argument against doing the talk show, as they saw it. It was my hope that it would be different, that I could be the focus of media attention for something other than my kidnapping, rather due to my own work. My intention was never to become famous; it just so happened that I was famous due to my circumstances. What would be so wrong about using my fame to do something meaningful, to provide myself with a foundation that I could build on? Naturally, this legiti-mate, but perhaps somewhat naïve view of things backfired on me.

After the channel had announced the format, many media outlets were already expressing initial scepticism, which did not go unnoticed by the channel's editorial department. We postponed the launch of the talk show, although the first couple interviews had already been recorded. Finally, the first interview was broadcast on 1 June 2008, reaching the highest market share to date. It was a success, certainly due to the curi-osity of a number of television viewers, who wanted to see how I fared.

In the responses to my interview with Austrian former Formula One driver Niki Lauda, who I had expressly wanted to talk to, my on-the-job performance was really just a side note. There was no "really well done" or "could have been much better"; no, the press issued a collective groan: "Now she feels she has to invade the television with her story as well. Can't you just stay home and cry her eyes out, like any normal person would?" However, the reactions I received by e-mail were completely

---

* Georg Danzer (1946-2007) was an Austrian singer-songwriter.

different. I received messages from well-wishers from as far away as Italy, who were happy that I had embarked on new adventures in efforts to restart my life.

The fact that the Austrian press still insisted on harping on my merely "mediocre" market share compared to the Austrian Broadcasting Corporation (ORF) – my talk show had been up against the thriller Collateral with Tom Cruise – put a damper on the project not just for me, but also for the channel. Following Niki Lauda, we broadcast the interviews with Stefan Ruzowitzky and Veronika Ferres. Ruzowitzky had just won the Oscar for Best Foreign Language Film with his movie The Counterfeiters (Die Fälscher ). I interviewed German actress Veronika Ferres at the hotel Bayerischer Hof in Munich on the margins of an event for her Power Child Foundation. She had just published a picture book about "stranger danger". The book was aimed at helping parents talk to their children about how to handle difficult situations. Specifically, the focus was on preventive measures, such as "don't talk to strangers", "don't take sweets from anyone" and "don't get in the car with anyone you don't know".

When I was a child the police had handed out pamphlets on this subject depicting the proper thing to do in such a situation and describing the evil intentions of such strangers. It was a bit strange to hear the pointers that were certainly essentially correct, but had not saved me from being kidnapped myself. Maybe the fact that the topic was too close to home was one of the reasons that the broadcast was not one of my top shows among the recorded pilots. Perhaps it was also because a cleaning lady kept running in front of the camera by accident and had to be edited out in a number of places. It was similar with Niki Lauda, where the air-conditioning unit was so loud and the lighting had to be constantly readjusted, because we felt like we were being barbecued alive and were practically glued to our stools for all of our sweating. It was just fine, and our ratings were, as I've already said, not bad at all.

In November 2008 we discussed a new direction for the format. The aim was to make it a bit more tabloid-esque, with more clip inserts, less static, more action. It was too bad, but perhaps the right decision even for me. A great deal of derision was expressed by a number of publications, which was to be expected. It was clear they couldn't handle it. Sometimes I think that if I had become famous as a result of "wardrobe malfunctions" that ended up displaying my nipples or bizarre performances on the Internet or in TV shows like I'm a Celebrity…Get Me Out of Here!, It is likely that fewer people would have been so indignant at giving me my own talk show. Perhaps they would have smiled resignedly, saying, "Oh well, another one of those starlets who thinks she's a star". I've never viewed myself that way. I've met celebrities at many events I was invited to who made it very clear to me that I was not one of them: "What are you doing here? You have achieved absolutely nothing. We have to bend over backwards to attract the spotlight, and you can do it without even trying."

This "without even trying" is something I have never sought. I simply had a naïve idea that I could build a bridge to something that I had always dreamt of as a child. I wanted to be self-employed and earn my own money. Perhaps as an actress, writing books, or doing something with the media or arts. If I didn't have my background as a kidnapping victim and had grown up completely "normally", nobody would complain or judge me that way for what I'm doing. It would be about my work pure and simple, and how good or bad it was. No value judgments, just an objective assessment.

On one hand I'm accused of commercializing myself with my story. When I look at the options I have been presented with over the last several years, at what doors were open to me, it must be said that there were very few of them. And in the end all of them certainly came back full circle to the "Kampusch case". A number of doors have been closed in my face for that very reason. Whenever I have "reduced" myself to my story on my own in my attempt to "reclaim my story, tell it from my perspective", it was very quickly used against me. Now she's parading her story across 284 pages of her book and is simply trying to make some quick cash with her self-pity tour. "And what about us. We pay taxes and scrape by, while she's sitting on her fat behind counting money. I don't think that she was really locked up, because it wouldn't be at all possible for someone to survive that."*

---

* Internet reaction to the publication of my book 3,096 Days

6

# 3,096 Days

## *My Book Is Made into a Film*

I would have liked to see more of how I survived. I wasn't that kind of victim. Moreover, there was no character development for either of the two main figures. But still, the film once again stirred a great deal up for me.

When Bernd Eichinger heard on the news in August 2006 that in Austria a girl, who had disappeared so long ago and spent so many years in captivity, had reappeared, he felt electrified. He ordered his office to collect every scrap of information on the case. You never know if it might become material for making a film.

Already shortly after my escape, Constantin Film issued a pro forma offer in order to secure the film rights. At the time nobody was thinking about anything like that, least of all me. I had enough to do with finding my footing in my new life. I did not find out that the offer had been made in the first place and that my attorneys were continually asked about it until I reached an agreement with Eichinger and Constantin Film early in the summer of 2010. The filming was to begin in 2011, and the movie was to be shown in cinemas one year later.

I was familiar with Eichinger's film productions, such as We Children from Bahnhof Zoo, The Name of the Rose, The House of the Spirits, Downfall or The Baader Meinhof Complex. All of them were very impressive and spectacularly produced films where a great deal of action took place. My story was different. There were no fast scene changes. Essentially there were only two scene settings (the dungeon and the house) and – aside from stories from my childhood – only two actors. Myself and the kidnapper. The story was about power and its abuse, about the relationship between criminal and victim. And about a rather subtle development, namely how unequal power relationships gradually come into balance, how I developed strategies to assure my survival. Strategies that finally helped me escape and survive the kidnapper. Understated material full of psychology, despite all of the drama that was inherent in my kidnapping case. It was more an intimate play, a tough tug-of-war, not a loud, action-packed film.

I was sceptical as to whether my story was the right material for him, or at least how I wanted it to be produced on screen. I had not been asked. Why would they? My advisors assured me that everything would be just fine. That Eichinger wanted to take the material on, was a genius, particularly as he wanted to write the script and direct the film himself. The material was predestined to be an Oscar winner, they said.

I wasn't even sure if I really wanted my story to be made into a movie. The work on my book that was supposed to form the foundation for the manuscript wasn't even finished yet.

All those months had sapped a great deal of my strength in confronting the whole story again. My childhood, my years of captivity and the period just after my escape. At times I felt that I had run up against the limits of what I could take. More than once I woke up startled after having fallen asleep on the couch, glancing around in panic because I thought I was back in the dungeon.

At the same time I wanted to tell my story to close the gaps, so that a great deal could no longer be kept a secret. I wanted to reclaim my past somewhat; after all there was no way I could run away from it. I wanted to regain control over the narrative of my experiences, which had taken on a life of its own in the meantime, undergoing constant reinterpretation and evaluation. For me, this book was also a kind of protective cover. When I was asked about the same things again and again, I could now point to the fact that I had written everything down between the two covers of my book, and that there was nothing more to say.

As difficult as it was, the work on my book helped me process my past. And it really helped people understand me a bit better, so that I did not have to always explain so much. No longer could others read a great deal into the period of my captivity, because the media now had to grapple with my view of things.

At the book presentation in Vienna in September 2010 I said that I hoped I could finally shed the "burdensome weight" of my past and finally begin to live my new life. While I was being hooked up with microphones in an adjacent room, a bookshop employee told me that there were around 700 people there spread out over two levels, and that the reading and the following Q&A would be shown on video screens. Television and radio teams had come from France and Germany, in addition to a number of journalists from the print media.

Those attending my reading had already patiently waited in line for hours between metal barricades and been subjected to bag checks. That morning the newspaper reported that over thirty security guards, several detectives and around sixty employees would be on hand to provide for my security and to ensure that the event would go off smoothly. Obvious fears of targeted disruption were more than just conjecture. On the Internet "Kampusch haters" had called for supporters to take appropriate action.

All of this was certainly not conducive to calming my nerves. During the reading I stumbled frequently in the beginning; it was a very important, but also very painful section of the book. It was about one day in 2004, where I was supposed to bake a cake according to a recipe from Priklopil's mother. I had read it through to myself several times so as not to make any mistakes. He stood behind me, commenting on every move I made. "My mother doesn't break the eggs that way at all." – "The cake is going to be a disaster anyway. I can see that already." – "Watch out! You are much too clumsy. The whole counter is covered in flour." No matter what I did, it was wrong, or provided him with another opportunity to compare my incapability to the infallibility of his mother. After the next hurtful comment I blurted, "If your mother can do everything so much better, why don't you ask her to bake you a cake?"

From one second to the next he lost control, swept the bowl with the cake batter from the counter, beat me with his fists and pushed me against the kitchen table. Then he dragged me down into the basement and turned the light off. Over the course of the next day I increasingly lost control over my body and my thoughts. I had cramps and tried to satisfy my persistent hunger by drinking water. To no avail. I couldn't think about anything other than eating something. And that I had crossed the line, that now he would really let me waste away in misery. I began to hallucinate, lying high up on my bunk bed whimpering and bathed in sweat, imagining myself on a slowly sinking ship. The water climbed higher and higher. It was cold. I felt it lapping at just my arms and legs, then at my chest and then at my neck.

At some point I heard the kidnapper's voice, followed by a thumping sound I could not place. "Here you go." Then silence again. Everything around me tilted. I had long lost any sense of space and time. Below me was nothingness, black nothingness, my hand reaching down into emptiness again and again. It took me an eternity for me to realize where I was and to gather the strength to grope for the ladder and carefully climb down backwards, rung by rung. When I had reached the floor, I crept forward on all fours until my hand bumped against a small plastic bag.

I ripped it open greedily, my fingers shaking. I was so clumsy that the contents of the bag fell out, rolling across the floor. In a panic, I groped around until I felt something long and cool. A carrot? I crawled around, searching every corner until I had collected a handful that I took back up to my bed. After I had wolfed down the carrots, one after the other, my stomach rumbled loudly, and was seized in cramps. It wasn't until two days later that the kidnapper came back, asking, "Are you going to be good now?"

When I had finished reading the passage, nobody in the audience moved a muscle. I had the feeling that everybody understood at that moment that there are various forms of abuse and of physical and psychological torment. Kidnapping and imprisoning someone already constitute an abuse per se. The kidnapper stole years of my life and any chance of normalcy. The hunger and humiliation I endured outweighed the public speculations. Looking over my entire eight and half years of captivity, that was just another piece of the puzzle.

After I escaped I sometimes had the feeling that being reduced to this one aspect was another form of abuse. Because it shrank the kidnapper's perfidious overall strategy down to the satisfaction of one psychological drive, making it sound as if he had perpetrated "only" this one crime against me. But really, there were so many more, whose impact I still feel today.

*

The idea of talking about these kinds of individual scenes, which only depict a small portion of the entire story, with a director who was a complete stranger to me, or even an entire film crew, was not an easy one for me. Particularly being opened up again, this time having to go perhaps even deeper than I had already in writing my book, where I was only confronted with the images in my own head. I was not eager to deal with all of this again. I had opened up so much in my book, while at the same time setting a limit that I hoped would be respected.

When a documentary about my ordeal was to be filmed as early as 2009[*], the focus going into the project was always on the possibility that I had not yet told the whole story. A story that the public absolutely had to know in order to understand exactly what had happened in those eight and half years. I believe that people will never be able to understand, because that period in my life goes beyond anyone's imaginative capacities. The kidnapper, who could have provided information on his motives and behaviour, had avoided making any kind of statement by committing suicide. I bear the entire burden of his incomprehensible deed on my shoulders. In many ways. I live with its consequences, including those that are so absurd that I never could have imagined them. I am asked to explain things I cannot explain. I am asked to justify things that are unjustifiable, to live up to an image that I do not want to live up to. Sometimes it's like a perversion of something Wolfgang Priklopil said, "You belong to me alone. I have created you."

Of course I have become a public person as a result of that person's actions. But only as a result of his actions. I did not go stand in front of Vienna's St. Stephen's Cathedral, calling out, "Look here. Here I am. Please let me be famous. I will tell you the whole story, from beginning to end." What I have told of the story is enough to understand what cannot really be understood. Very seldom have journalists asked for questions on the abuse I suffered, my forced semi-starvation, the mental and physical violence that I was subjected to for eight and half years. In an interview I once said that it seems to me sometimes as if some of the "spectators" were waiting for games like those in ancient Rome. If I were the cynical type, I would ask if the spectacle was somehow not enough. Does there have to be even more? If there were more, how would that

---

[*] Broadcast in 2010 as 3096 Tage Gefangenschaft (3,096 Days of Captivity)

change things? Nothing changes in the life of the "spectators". Those who are confronted with it for just a short period of time – the police officers, the judges, the public. For them it's just a criminal case. A story that gives you the creeps, that appals you, or whatever.

I am not willing to open up every corner of my inner being to public scrutiny. And I don't understand why people keep demanding that I do exactly that. It would neither help clear up the case, which has already been solved, even though some people are still unwilling to accept that. And it would not add anything to the kidnapper's punishment, which he managed to avoid by killing himself. Even if some people refused to accept his suicide and even suspect murder. It would also not allow me to better process all of those terrible years, for people to treat me differently. It would only serve to satisfy a strange desire that I would not even call hunger for sensationalism.

In the Fritzl case, which would later often be mentioned in the same breath as mine, much of this was not an issue because everything was already on the table. There was a criminal who soaked up a lot of the attention. There was a daughter who had been abused, for years. An incestuous, coercive relationship that produced children who had to be protected. The issue was not an issue. It was plain that nobody need know the details.

As I said, there are many forms of abuse. There is mental cruelty, but nothing seems to weigh as heavily and to fan the flames of people's imaginations as much as sexual abuse. In the British yellow press I was christened "the sex slave" for years, and in German-language tabloids the kidnapper was dubbed "the sex beast". That sick man was indeed in many ways a beast, but that is apparently not enough. Of course I was also subjected to sexual assault, but the fact that I have spoken and written about it is apparently not enough. And "they" are certainly not able to deal with the fact that I have always stressed that I wanted to preserve at least a shred of privacy. Many people seem to think that it is my duty in particular to inform the public about every tiny detail of my

116

story, every episode, every emotion. The constant demands to reveal even more, as if they wanted to deprive me of my rights to individuality and privacy a second time. That is exactly what the kidnapper did for eight and half years.

Why is my desire for at least this small shred of privacy so difficult to understand and accept? Most people, particularly if they've gained a certain level of notoriety, do not like it at all when they are asked in an interview or an article about their school grades or when their salary is published. But I'm supposed to shine light into the darkest corners of my story and I'm scolded when I refuse to do so. They point out in a supposedly well-meaning way that refusing to do so leaves room for speculation. And if I wished to prevent speculation, I would simply have to spit out the whole truth. Who really wants to know the scope of my truth so precisely?

Additionally, I have learned the very bitter lesson that these speculations will never stop. Because the crime in and of itself goes beyond the human imagination, which is why people apparently feel the need to continue to garnish and embellish it while indulging in the most far-fetched theories. Because the relationship between the victim and the kidnapper is so complex, because there is no clear black or white. Because society needs such supposed monsters like Wolfgang Priklopil in order to put a face on the evil that resides within it, thereby separating out the evil from its midst. It needs images of cellar dungeons so as not to have to see the well-tended façades and front yards where violence hides behind a fully normal, middle-class appearance. Wolfgang Priklopil was a man who was described by his neighbours as friendly, helpful and perhaps a bit shy. After the fact they pretended that they had always felt something was a bit off. He was a bit strange yes, but something like that? No, unthinkable. Still, he was a human being, not a beast. That would be too easy. We are all shaped by our environment. Nobody is born into this world completely evil. We all have our personal histories, but people don't want to see that. Otherwise they would have to do too

117

much soul-searching of their own. There are thousands of victims of supposed every day crimes, thousands of abused people, most of them women and children, but others as well. And all of this takes place in the very everyday prison of their own homes or in children's own bedrooms.

There are probably thousands of diary entries like this that, however, are never made public:

*Punches and kicks, choking, scratching, bruising my wrist, squeez-ing of the same, shoving against the door frame. Beating me in and around my stomach with a hammer and fists. Bruises on: my right hip bone, right upper and lower arm, my left and right thigh and my shoulders. Abrasions and scratches on my thighs, my left calf. Pummelling me several times, black bruises below my shoulder blades and along my spine. He hit me on my right ear, still feel only stabbing pain and hear only crackling noises. Then he continued to hit me on the head.*

Crimes like the one perpetrated against me help to cement the frame-work of good and evil that supports our society. Their abnormality helps us to direct our gaze from normal, everyday madness to the extremes. They help us to differentiate where so many shades of grey are. The kid-napper must be perverse and inhuman, so that we can remain human ourselves. As a result, the crime becomes something so far apart from us that it is completely divorced from our own lives.

From the very beginning I have spoken openly about this aspect, about the need for differentiation. But as soon as I tried to sketch out a more nuanced image, even of the kidnapper, the lines between good and evil start to blur for many people. That must not be allowed. The world is complex enough, and we want to have clarity on this one point. Evil personified must not be allowed to have any kind of human side whatso-ever. Otherwise evil can no longer be externalized.

In my case the question of how people in our midst can escape any kind of controls is hardly addressed. Today it is brought up perhaps more often where we are looking at other cases, such as Amstetten, or now very recently in Höxter, a town in the German state of North Rhine-Westphalia. Here as well the criminals seemed quite normal to the outside world, as inconspicuous as the façades of their homes.

It is apparent that something is wrong in our society. But before we take a closer look, we prefer to salaciously give ourselves over to speculating about what could have happened behind closed doors. It seems to always be more interesting to train our gaze outward as opposed to inward. What goes on on the "inside" of those involved is largely deemed unimportant. In some ways this applies to the criminal, but often enough also to the victim.

People often only express their affection for the victim if they can feel superior or sympathize. During my captivity I often wondered what it would be like. If I showed everybody how terrible things were for me, how much I suffered, would they ever be able to see me as a "normal person" again? Would I be condemned to victim status for eternity?

After my escape and my first interview I received a flood of letters from people who expressed their genuine and honest compassion. They were not experiencing any internal conflict and had no expectations of me, whatever those might be. But I also received a large number of other letters. From people who accused me of not knowing what suffering looks like, because if I had truly experienced suffering, I would have to be broken. One anonymous letter writer even scolded me writing, "You who have debased yourself so, what are you doing up here with us? You need to stay down there in your dirty swamp, down there far away, because that's where you belong!"

But really, what does a broken person look like? Who would dare take it upon themselves to sit in judgment on that? If I had been broken by my isolation, I would not have survived my captivity. And only because I don't go around talking about how badly I am doing sometimes, how dark some days are, doesn't mean that I don't have such days. For me, every new day is a balancing act. Testing the waters of what I can manage today and what I can't. Whether I feel confident enough to go out in public or whether I would rather hide out in my flat. A couple of years ago I went through a phase where I began to reject the world outside. That world that I had looked forward to so much and had associated with so many positive thoughts and possibilities. For part of that world I was somewhat of a provocation. Perhaps because I perplexed it with the way I dealt with my abduction and my captivity. Maybe I trigger so much aggression because the kidnapping triggers aggression. And because I'm the only person who is here within reach, I am the only one on the receiving end of that aggression. Not the kidnapper, who actually deserves it. I had to learn that much of the rejection that was directed at me had nothing to do with me, but rather that many people experience forms of violence that they were unable to escape from. Because they have not yet processed their experiences or are stuck every day in their own prison and cannot break free, although in fact the door is standing wide open. Just like in my case, their mental prison is stronger. The fact that after several years I have managed to overcome both doors perhaps makes their own powerlessness painfully obvious.

That has nothing to do with me, but in some cases I have to come to terms with the open hate and rejection. I was able to muster up my defences to counter the terror and the dark fantasies of the kidnapper to prevent myself from being broken. Now the world wanted to see exactly that. A broken person, still constantly dependent on help from others. I spent so many years being dependent on a person who would come, open the heavy door in order to toss a couple of carrots into my dungeon; on a person who would allow me out of the dungeon for a couple of hours in accordance with his rules and thanks to his mercy. Because of this I longed for almost nothing more than no longer having to be needy and dependent.

*

Both the kidnapper and I underwent all of these interconnections and stages of development, and that was my intention in writing my book 3,096 Days. I was surprised at the positive feedback and at the fact that people liked the book – inasmuch as it is possible to like reading about such subject matter. The people who read my book told me that they had all of a sudden felt that they were close to me, that they understood me. For me, it was like I had given people a piece of myself, providing courage and hope without having to expose myself in an unpleasant way. One lady said to me, "Before I didn't know what to think of you. But now that I've read the book, you have my utmost respect." There is no greater praise than that. The book not only gave me back the power to define my narrative, but also lent me a kind of seriousness, allowing people to better understand how I was able to present myself so clearly and thoughtfully after my escape.

*

Precisely these aspects – shedding light on various stages of development – was supposed to be the focus of the movie as I saw it. And that was precisely my attitude when I met with Bernd Eichinger for the first time.

In the early part of the summer in 2010 there were several meetings in Vienna at the Hotel Imperial Café that I did not attend. Our first meeting was to take place in an open-gallery office on the Ringstrasse boulevard that provides a wonderful view of the Stadtpark. Eichinger had been described to me as "difficult", a bit macho, someone who knew what he wanted and was able to get it. It turned out later that he had heard similar reports about me. It seems that we had both rolled up our sleeves and were not prepared to move a single inch from our own ideas. And that is exactly how our first meeting went. We were both staking out our territory, jockeying over who would have the upper hand. It was my story, but he was the famous director who wanted to film it.

After a couple minutes of unimportant small talk about the weather and the beautiful view, we got right to the point. The manuscript of my book, which was not yet quite finished, was "not bad at all", a good basis for a film script, but … I wanted to know what was lacking in his opinion. Well, everything really that I had not talked about openly to date, but most certainly had to be there.

I felt like I was in a scene from a terrible movie and reacted accordingly. Dismissive, defensive, a bit hostile. Why did he have to start off with what he called gaps? Why not tackle what we already had?

After two hours, the project appeared to be dead. Angrily he stomped down the stairs, stating that if I didn't want to talk, there was no basis for the project, and that he couldn't work that way. For several minutes I sat in the office alone. Did that now mean victory or defeat? Had I driven off an opponent or a partner who took an honest interest in working up my story?

Later on I found out that Eichinger was indeed irritated and a bit perplexed, and that he had drowned his frustration in a number of drinks at the Hotel Imperial, but also that he had never seriously decided to throw in the towel at any time. He was not going to give up that easily. It was really only logical that I reacted so negatively. It was not without reason that I was mistrustful, even fearful of being dictated again by someone else, of losing control. I was not able to simply trust in the fact that everything would turn out just fine. The fact that everything would not automatically "be just fine" was something that I had learned quite painfully from my more recent past.

There was radio silence for several weeks. Eichinger had gone back to the US, where he apparently continued to think about implementing the project despite my hostile attitude. That fall, after the work on my book was completed, I received an invitation to his Austrian home at Lake Wolfgang. It was pouring down rain, and my companion and I kept missing the right turn-off. We were very clearly late to our appointment. On the mobile: "No, now you've gone much too far!" – "Where are you now? Can you see the campground? Now drive toward ..." - We were guided to his house. Fortunately our lateness was not an issue. After a brief tour we were treated to a delicious cherry strudel, and that evening we sat by the fireplace and talked.

It was a cautious attempt at finding common ground. Step-by-step each of us was prepared to abandon the role that we both had played up to that point. The next day was when the real work began. His first question focused on the beginning of that fateful day: He wanted to know exactly what details had triggered my morning argument with my mother. I told him about the evening before, when my father had brought me home much later than agreed and had failed to accompany me to the apartment door, not looking to get into it with my mother. "Jesus Christ! You are hours late. How can he allow you to cross the courtyard alone in the middle of the night? God knows what could've happened to you. I'll tell you one thing: You will not see your father again. I'm so tired of this, and I will not stand for it any longer!"

I told him about the next morning and about other situations where I was forced to take sides, to favour one over the other. Again and again he interrupted me saying, "I need to be able to imagine this exactly." The part where my mother came into my room once again on the evening before the kidnapping in order to lay out my clothes for the next day and to caress my head briefly seem to be a key moment for him, an attempt at reconciliation. I turned away and pulled the blanket over my head. The next morning, after she slapped my cheek, I said goodbye to the cats, but not to my mother. I was not going to give her a kiss; I was going to punish her by giving her the silent treatment.

Eichinger was so immersed in what had happened that I had the feeling that he wanted to slowly peel away the layers of the people behind this "case". He was examining interaction on a number of levels and not focusing on a foregrounded spectacle. He worked his way forwards in the story, largely chronologically, up until my first few weeks in the dungeon.

Sometime after I returned to Vienna, I received an invitation to another round of discussions at his house by the lake. We had to interrupt our talks on a number of occasions, because I was unable to go on, or he needed to "catch a breath of fresh air" in order to sort through what he had heard. On our last evening he laid out for me in great detail how he envisaged the film. He wanted to expose the core underpinning of the human actions and pour it into a mould that he could use to explain the incomprehensible. It was to be a radical film in which he wanted to "completely rethink" its dimensions. A kind of lifting of boundaries of both mind and space, as conveyed in images – although conceivably there was hardly any other more limited space than my dungeon and the interplay between kidnapper and victim. Filmed in 3-D in order to allow the viewers to experience the immediacy of the closeness, the distance, the reality and fantasy worlds.

That sounded a little bit abstract, but he explained very sensitively and patiently to me that he saw my kidnapping as more than just a classic criminal case. He was fascinated primarily by the development that I had undergone all those years. From being absolutely inferior, slowly attaining equal footing, and then gaining the strength of a survivor. He wanted to turn the domestic setting into a battlefield, on which the drama between the kidnapper and the victim, as well as the drama between the kidnapper and his mother played out. The dictates of orderliness and cleanliness were to become a tool of oppression, to expose the cruelty that we would not expect to be hidden behind properly trimmed hedgerows, but in actuality took place precisely there.[*]

---

[*] See also: Katja Eichinger, BE, dtv, 2014, p. 562.

*

After our first, rather intimidating encounter, I felt that Eichinger was a strong person, full of life, with a sensitive and warm-hearted side. At Christmas he sent me a package from the US with a CD collection of the Beatles, because I had casually mentioned once that I like their music so much. I cut our last phone call short because I – ironically enough – was on my way to the movies. When I received the call at the end of January 2011 that he had collapsed at a restaurant in Los Angeles and had died, I found it impossible to believe at first.

For a long time nobody knew whether the project was to be continued, and if so, then how. I was familiar with portions of the script that he had completed up until that time; everything that he had explained to me had been written down, line for line. The story of an illusion, wary, subtle and for exactly that reason conveying an enormous power.

The movie itself contains none of Eichinger's ideas or the fragments of his script. The new director, Sherry Hormann, made it very clear to me at our first meeting that she intended to make her own film. That is certainly legitimate, but I did not realize just how far she would go until I saw the finished product at the advance screening. The film contained scenes that I had talked about only in the context of my police interviews. And scenes that even went beyond those. Hormann had neither integrated or embedded them in order to make them comprehensible in any way. She did not tell a story, it was not an intimate play, and the characters underwent zero development. Nothing was subtle; everything was obvious and wooden.

At the first press conference to discuss the film project I had said that the many sympathetic letters I had received over the last two years had encouraged me to make a movie version of my story. And that I was happy that an extraordinary opportunity had arisen with Bernd Eichinger and Constantin Film in taking a very sensitive and deft approach to bringing my story to the screen.

Nothing of that came out in the end. I was disappointed and felt that my trust had been abused. My story had escaped my grasp once more. So many scenes had been rendered so heavy-handedly that I wondered exactly what effect the movie meant to achieve. Is it always necessary to use a sledgehammer for people to get the point? In doing so, in a way you deny people the capability of thinking and feeling for themselves and forming their own opinion.

The way I had dealt with my story in interviews or even in my book actually should have been evidence that discretion was important to me. I would never say, "Everybody look at how skinny I am and how much he humiliated me. That doesn't bother me in the least." Of course parts of the film reflected my reality. Of course I had been starved down to skin and bones, was most often scantily clothed and had been forced to be humiliated by him in various ways, including physical assault. But that was one facet of my eight and half years. And the film focused solely on that. The film doesn't make you understand the demons that drove Priklopil. You can't understand the relationship that grew out of our situation. The life that I was forced to live in that house and in that dungeon was not explained in the least. That was exactly the point, and not to show a rape scene for minutes on end. At the time one film critic wrote very accurately, "The viewer is forced to become a voyeur against his will. The rape scenes evoke discomfort."*

What pained me in particular was that there was no development to be seen. At least a number of reviewers faulted the film for that: "Hormann demonstrated little ability to convey much of anything of the energy to survive that Natascha Kampusch drew on to gradually free herself from the hole in the cellar and to widen her margin of manoeuvre with her tormentor."** Another wrote, Hormann does not play on our

---

* http://www.br.de/br-fernsehen/sendungen/kino-kino/3096-tage-kampusch-entfueh-rung-film-filmkritik-100.html (Version: August 2016)
** http://derstandard.at/1361241090000/Annaeherung-an-ein-Langzeitverbrechen (Version:Au-

emotions. She does not delve into psychology. And she avoids creating the necessary backdrop that would explain the actions perpetrated by Priklopil."*

The film exposed me and was built on images and scenes that stemmed from fantasies and not from the reality as I had lived it. The director announced in an interview that these kinds of details had of course become well known based on my police interview records, that the issue of sexuality presented itself "unavoidably" and that the scenes were "of course not filmed in a sensationalistic manner, but the way they were". However, the script author's position was revealing: "Images are layered over perception – perhaps even Ms. Kampusch's internal perception itself. We naturally thought it our duty to do justice to her. [...] We of course invented some scenes the way we understood them."**

Here again, the truth is apparently not sordid enough and requires further embellishment. And why, pray tell, should other people's fantasies be layered over my own images? Because they are incorrect? But ok, I sold the film rights, which meant that the film crew had the freedom to make its own movie.

*

When the film was finally shown to an audience at its premiere, I snuck out of the theatre after just a few minutes. I had participated in the premier because it was an imperative out of courtesy to bring this project, which had begun with Eichinger, properly to an end, even though I did not feel comfortable with the finished product. At the time I refrained from expressing open criticism. That would have seemed unfair to me. After all, the actors had delivered a good and convincing performance within the framework that was available to them.

Sitting with so many people in a movie theatre while the images moved across the screen in front of me was more difficult for me than watching the film on my own. I felt a strange distance between myself and the film, between myself and the people sitting there, but also a closeness at the same time that I found difficult to handle.

This was primarily due to the fact that the film set was very authentic. A replica of the dungeon had been built at the Bavaria Filmstudios. They had found on site locations that were very similar in size and furnishing for a number of scenes upstairs in the house or in my mother's apartment. I visited the set once or twice and also met the actors. It was disconcerting to be there with them. These were my spaces, and yet they weren't. It was like encountering myself, my mother and my kidnapper, and in a way it wasn't. Everything was very tangible and very abstract.

Amelia Pidgeon, who played young Natascha, really did look quite a bit like me. The first time we met she gave me a stuffed squirrel and said, "if I were ever kidnapped, I would like to know how to survive it. And that's why I want to play this role."

There was one incident with Thure Lindhardt, who played Wolfgang Priklopil, where I almost felt sorry for him. Between the trailers, where the actors went to rest or to freshen up, there were a number of folding tables and benches with hot dogs and other snacks and drinks. The afternoon that I was there someone had brought in a giant cake from a bakery. Thure cut the cake and was just about to pass around pieces of cake on plates. But before he was able to even put his fork in the cake, a voice from one of the trailers bellowed, "You want an even stricter diet plan?!" Even though he already was so thin. However, that would have been a truly authentic scene much in the way it might have happened during my captivity.

128

# 7

# *"Perhaps I Will Destroy the House One Day with Explosives"*

## *The House in Strasshof*

Again and again I see that flowers or votive candles have been placed in front of the fence, with small notes and prayers, some of them even for the kidnapper. There were also telephone calls saying that Wolfgang Priklopil had been a good person and that in truth I had murdered him.

The first time that I was confronted with the "real" place of my captivity again, with the house I was locked up in for so long, was through the television. I had escaped just a few days before when the images of a crime scene inspection flickered across the screen. Men in white suits, a camera team, all trying to squeeze themselves into my small dungeon, touching my things and affixing numbers to them.

You could see the oppressive confinement of the small space. On the right-hand side was the double sink, next to it the toilet with the Donald Duck lid. In the beginning the toilet had a beige lid which had been ruined when I placed a hot pan on it once by mistake. So that the kidnapper wouldn't immediately notice that I had destroyed something "wilfully", I papered over the crack in the lid with a sticker of a horse. I don't remember whether he punished me after he noticed it anyway. I only remember that I was very happy when I received my new, pretty, colourful toilet lid with Donald wearing a diving mask for my birthday.

The Allibert bathroom cabinet with my toothbrush and toothpaste, hand cream, my hairbrush, a nail file made from cardboard with roughed up surfaces and rounded points so that I couldn't hurt him or me with it. Above the mirrored cabinet there was a shelf containing my red swivelled cassette tape holder, several folders and the book Schülerwissen. Next to that was a small rack for drying laundry.

The second bookshelf and the black hanging cabinet that I had decorated with colourful stickers, small arts and crafts, pictures and poems that were important to me. The small desk, above it the shelf with the television and the radio. In the hanging cabinet above my desk were over-the-counter medical supplies, a number of novels, a transparent Plexiglas box with my passport in the bottom, which led to a great deal of speculation. Actually it had originally been in the inner pocket of my red parka, because I had returned from my trip to Hungary with my father the evening just before my kidnapping. With all the bickering about me coming home late my mother had forgotten to take it out of my jacket. A coincidence, nothing more, and not any kind of evidence that I had planned my "disappearance" in any way.

On left hand side against the wall was the bunk bed, a couple of articles of clothing on the metal ladder. Across from the heavy door was a hook with the dress I had worn on the day of my abduction. Over the years, as I grew, I had taken it apart and turned the bottom of the dress into a skirt with an elastic waistband. I always put it on at Christmas because I wanted to wear something nice. It wasn't until several years ago that I was able to get that dress back from the police, along with a number of other personal items, after repeated requests.

I believe it is the right approach to keep a number of items in the evidence room in the hopes of being able to bring additional clarity to the crime with the help of new technologies. The crime perpetrated against me was essentially solved, at least from my point of view. Traces of two kinds of DNA were found on my personal things and in the dungeon. Mine and the kidnapper's. Upstairs in the house were also traces of the kidnapper, including traces of his mother, and a few of mine as well. What additional information could my dress have provided? Or poems and drawings? They reflected my state of mind, but nothing more. The few diary entries I wrote proved the abuse that I was subjected to. At the time I did not document all of the insanity extensively and seamlessly because I believed that that would provide the kidnapper with more of a target for attacking me. What if he found my writing and read it?

The few times when I actually did write over a longer period of time it was primarily to keep myself focused on reality. So that my very few positive experiences, which I naturally clung to in my thoughts, would not paper over the cruelties I was subjected to for years. It was an attempt to readjust the dimensions of my life. After all Priklopil had hammered into me over the years that he was only doing what was best for me. He was protecting me, and he was there when nobody else was. I wanted to put it down in black and white that that was untrue. That he was wrong, that he was not my saviour, but my tormentor. The man who had taken my old life from me.

All of these things that were seized at the time were not able to explain anything about the kidnapper's motives. Nothing about possible masterminds in the background, who have fuelled speculation even to this day, albeit no longer so loudly after all of the evaluation commissions. The notes on the abuses I suffered, which I had painstakingly detailed during several days in August 2005 primarily, because this was a phase of particular violence, could have aggravated a criminal sentence if there had been somebody to condemn for it. But the kidnapper had long since issued his own judgment.

In a way it was hurtful to watch all of those strangers turning the room where I lived upside down. How disrespectfully they handled items that were very important to me, items I spent weeks fighting for. Of course I understood that the house had a separate meaning for the investigators and all of the others who were moving about the house and the dungeon: This was the place that the girl had been locked up in, the place that the kidnapper had created below ground specifically to commit that crime. It was a crime scene that had to be inspected meticulously.

For me that place meant something more. It wasn't just the scene of a kidnapping, but necessarily the room I had lived in. Even the dungeon, which for everybody was the epitome of cruelty, did not carry only that meaning for me. In the beginning I nearly went crazy in the darkness, the confinement, the cold. I was afraid that I would suffocate if he turned off my oxygen supply from upstairs. The fan and its scraping noise terrorized me. However, those five square metres were also my refuge. Here I could read something, listen to a cassette tape, do my arts and crafts and have peace and quiet. For me reading was like being part of the world. It was the only world that I had within my grasp for a long time. With the help of books I was able to go on adventure travels without having to leave the dungeon. Treasure Island or Kontiki were my stories of escape. The bunk bed became my look-out tower, a ship's rigging or a mountain peak. It was a journey I took purely in my head, but it worked.

Whenever I was alone down there, he could only use violence against me indirectly. The dungeon was just as much, or little, a place of hate as the house above it. Essentially, both of them were primarily places that are neutral in a manner of speaking. They are only filled with the energy of the people who inhabit them. They become the theatre for their ideas. In this case, these were the kidnapper's cruel and inhumane ideas. And my attempts to counter those with something different.

The dungeon had become my space because someone else had designed it for me. So it was up to me to try to conquer it for myself and fill it with my energy.

*

After the police had cleared the house as a crime scene and my attorneys and I had decided to join the court case as co-plaintiffs, I visited the house for the first time again. The inspection of the house in Strasshof together with an expert was scheduled for 10 AM.

It was a "local crime scene inspection" as it is called. Here as well it was apparently not possible to allow for even a bit of protection for the victim. The street was cordoned off, and a sea of journalists were outside, calling out, pushing and shoving and taking pictures. The few meters it took for me to reach the house were torturous. Aside from that, I was very tense, because I didn't know how the confrontation with my very recent past would go. Whether I would be able to withstand the pressure of my memories.

I looked past the privet hedgerow that reminded me of the vitality of the world outside after two years of my isolation in the dungeon. In December 2000 he allowed me to step out into the garden for just a few minutes for the first time after weeks of "preparation". "If you scream, I will kill you. If you run, I will kill you. I will kill anybody who either hears or sees you, if you are dumb enough to attract their attention." For the first time since my kidnapping I felt blades of grass and the soft ground beneath my feet. For the first time I inhaled the almost sharp, fresh air into my lungs, and the odour of mould and loneliness slowly gave way to the tangy scent of the privet hedgerow. I picked a couple of leaves and put them in my pocket. Just a few days later they had already turned brown and wilted. Still, I kept them in a small box.

We crossed the stone pavement driveway and entered the house. A yellow single-family dwelling with a slate roof, a dormer window, two chimneys and a satellite dish on the roof, the muntin windows with white edging, the roll-top shutters down halfway. Glass blocks above the white garage door. A house just like millions of others. Everything orderly; even the grass had not grown too high in the meantime.

Next to the wrought iron garden gate there was a brass doorbell plaque with an intercom system. On the other end of the stone pavement walkway, three steps with a black railing leading up to the main entrance with a semicircular transom window. I had never entered the house from this direction.

Once in the house, I ran wildly through all of the rooms. The bouquet of flowers his mother had brought on her last visit was still on the table in the living room with the dark wall unit, the heavy dark green leather couch and the red brick fireplace. Bananas and tomatoes were lying on a tray in the kitchen. A pile of newspapers were stacked up on the kitchen table in front of the birch forest wallpaper; a number of them had slipped off and were covering the table. He had terrorized me again and again with the orange kitchen scale on the wall, asking whether I was too stupid to measure decagrams and grams, whether I was capable of anything, and telling me that his mother could measure flour and sugar my "eyeing" the right amount anyway. The edge of the L-shaped kitchen counter that he would always shove me against if something had not gone to his liking when I was cooking or baking.

In the rustic "Jägerstüberl" room with the boar's hide hanging on the wall that had remained unchanged since the death of Priklopil's father you could see the traces of the kidnapper's highflying plans. A corner bathtub, a large heating unit, sinks, all waiting to be installed in the new bathroom. During my captivity I had laboured for months on the upper floor of the house, which contained three rooms. In addition, he wanted to finish the attic, to clad the rudimentary wooden construction with gypsum wallboard and to turn the room into a second living room. We broke through the ceiling between the first floor and the attic and installed an additional set of stairs with marble tiling. He never let handymen into the house not even for this very physical labour or for work that required technical skills, like installing heating units. At the time I was 12 years old when I carried cement bags, stripped doors, hammered holes in walls with a chisel. It was mercilessly physical labour, but after years of the limited environment in the dungeon, it offered a change of scenery and pace that marked the beginning of a new phase where he allowed me more freedom to "make myself useful" around the house.

During my captivity the entire house had seemed so intimidatingly powerful. So enormous and dark. The living room seemed to be even worse after my first visit back when inspecting the crime scene. The quintessence of middle-class, normal. Tasteful, weighty, oppressive and disconcerting in its entire posh-like splendour complete with wood panelling, a wall-length shelving unit and fireplace. The kitchen on the other hand, which for me had always been a place of intense humiliation, seemed almost harmless.

I was most afraid of the hallway leading to the garage and down into the dungeon. A bundle of flax for sealing off pipes hung over the workshop pit. Every time when I came up the stairs, handcuffed to the kidnapper, I had seen that light yellow bundle hanging up there. As if a wig of my own hair that he had shaved off my head were hanging up there. You mustn't leave any traces behind.

Surprisingly enough, I did not feel the anxiety I expected when we entered the garage. It was rather strange feeling of melancholy. That was perhaps because that I had only ever entered this room, supposedly secured by booby-traps, when I was allowed to go up into the hermetically sealed world of the house. After all, it was one step closer to freedom.

*

135

When the issue was discussed much later on in the media of whether I would sue the Republic of Austria for damages as a result of the errors in the police investigation during my captivity, my attorneys informed me that I was entitled to compensation from the estate of the kidnapper. It was a strange feeling, but one that brought about a bit of closure. After all he had robbed me of several years of my life. Why should I not be entitled to a portion of his estate? Psychologically speaking, he had taken so much from me that nothing in the world, no "valuables" could compensate for that. Certainly nothing of material value or of any other kind of value. Nevertheless, the newspapers were full of presumptuous commentaries and cartoons. Now she wants to file a lawsuit! She's already swimming in money. She simply can't get enough. And now she wants the house on top of all that?

What golden bathtub could I sit in like Scrooge McDuck, what shower of money raining down on me could give me back my adolescence, my "second life"? I sometimes wonder whether people heap such scorn and envy on lottery winners who come into money unexpectedly. What is the point of discussing whether compensation – no matter what shape or form – is justified or appropriate? How much is a year of your life worth? How much is a year of your life worth spent in torture and humiliation, locked away in a bunker? Not one cent, not even millions can make up for it. And anybody who had followed my story unbiased and free of judgment also knows that money was never my motivation. That the money I have received from donations or the sale of rights to my story has not only been used for me, but for charity purposes. The fact that accusations of unjustified enrichment are raised again and again is cynical and deeply hurtful. It shows that some people believe that money can sort everything out. A small, soothing consolation prize is not something that she needs to have, she already has enough. I am the one, not the kidnapper, who has been given a "life sentence".

We reached an agreement with the mother of Wolfgang Priklopil that I was to be granted the house from the estate. I did not file a lawsuit against the Republic of Austria. It would likely have led to years of legal disputes, and you could already see the beginning contours of what excesses that could lead to.

I have become a homeowner, also because I did not want the house to fall into the wrong hands. I could not have stood for transforming that house into a kind of chamber of horrors or a place of pilgrimage for strange people who secretly harbour admiration for the kidnapper and his crime. I know from the insults levelled at me on the Internet, letters delivered to me, interviews with political leaders and representatives of the judicial system, notes sometimes hanging on the garden fence of the house that these people exist. Some of them are people who knew the kidnapper when he was young, who have difficulty believing that he did what he did, and who pray that he can find his way back to the straight and narrow path in the afterlife. After all, because he was such a nice, polite young man. Others know exactly what happened. That a precocious 10-year-old planned her kidnapping herself, dragging a respectable young man with a slight personality disorder down into the abyss and coercing him into committing this crime.

Those are the moments where words simply fail me. You can't counter opinions like these with arguments. Not even with the truth. After all, because it cannot be verified, because the truth came from me.

Seen from a different angle, all this certainly takes on an aura of grotesqueness, that I must now pay electricity and water bills, not to mention property taxes, for a building I never wanted to live in. That somebody has to monitor the house regularly, check the heating and air it out. In the first several years I could not do that myself. A team of horses could not have dragged me back there. I also could not have managed to change anything in the house or in the garage. Not one screw, not one bucket of paint, not one book, not one vase was to be removed from its spot or even thrown away. As if I had to preserve it until I was ready to fill the house up entirely with myself.

The "ravages of time" finally dictated that I had to act. A storm had

137

torn several shingles from the roof, moisture had gotten into the house, and mould had begun to grow in several corners. The hedges urgently needed trimming, and the swimming pool in the garden had become a biotope for moss. "An eyesore", as many certainly said under their breath. I went to the house with a team of friends to clean it out; old furnishings and the remnants of renovation materials that could no longer be used were placed in a container. Experts were responsible for removing the moisture from the house and sprayed the particularly affected rooms with a special substance. Neighbours alerted the press. The photograph of me in a smock standing in front of debris and covered in dust bore the caption: "Is she now moving back into her house of horrors?"

*

A municipal decision was issued in 2013 requiring the dungeon to be filled in. Unapproved hollow spaces below the zero line are not permitted under the Lower Austrian Building Code. Understandably enough there had been no construction permit issued for my dungeon. It had been constructed illegally, and so as to avoid endangering public safety and to at least retroactively comply with the statutory provisions, the entire subterranean area was to be filled in. The hollow space was to be filled with around 18 cubic metres of coarse gravel, according to the expert jargon.

The police and the Lower Austrian Criminal Police Office had already used ground-penetrating radar during their first inspections of the crime scene to determine that the area had a number of shafts that were connected to my prison either directly or indirectly. Excavation work in the garden behind the house uncovered a half meter of ceiling constructions made from concrete, gravel and iron parts in a number of areas, a half-metre below the topsoil. To this day it has not been definitively

138

determined whether or not parts of the subterranean construction had been there long before the kidnapper had devised his plan to kidnap me.

Bringing in the course gravel was easier said than done. Through the garage, down into the workshop pit, through the small tunnel behind the safe – here you could only crawl through backwards – through the small anteroom to the dungeon: This would only be possible with buckets and shovels. The same applied to opening up the ventilation shaft from above. The only solution was to tear open the dungeon from the outside. A local construction company was contracted to do the work.

The next day a construction worker began hammering an enormous hole into the floor of the garage with heavy hammers. The noise attracted curious neighbours. One said, "Ah, you're finally filling in the bunker?" As if it had been widely known that a subterranean world had already been there long before. By that evening, after about ten hours of work, a 30 to 40 centimetre hole had been hammered into the concrete, but the ceiling of the dungeon was nowhere in sight. The next day, heavy equipment was brought in. A jackhammer pounded away for hours, the noise permeating the neighbourhood. That afternoon, the ceiling finally fell in. It was over a half a meter below the floor level. It was 60 centimetres thick and was made from cement, sand, metal bars and fist-size stones. The kidnapper could not have constructed this by himself. There was nothing slapdash about it like the interior of the installation. This was the work of professionals. Did nobody from the local authorities really know that a bunker was located on the property? Perhaps long before Priklopil's parents built the house on the undeveloped property?

The cellar surrounding the dungeon was cleared out. Shelving, buckets of paint, skis, tools that I had held in my hand while renovating the house, were disposed of. All of the remaining items still in the dungeon were brought up. The construction workers threw everything into a pile. The shelf where I had placed my soap and toothbrush broke apart after a strong kick, as did the Allibert bathroom cabinet. At least I was able to rescue the hook where my blue and white chequered dress had hung all those years. On top of the pile representing the second phase of my life was the torn picture of Don Bosco that I had pinned to my bulletin board. He probably would've said, "Go on. Leave all the junk there and try to grow fresh flowers on this pile of manure."

After the dungeon was filled in with gravel, the access stairs via the workshop pit and the anteroom in front of the steel reinforced door to my dungeon were filled in with concrete. In addition to the relief I felt that closure, in the true sense of the word, had been reached, another emotion rose to the surface of my consciousness. A kind of surreal, and yet painful grief and a goodbye to a very formative period in my life. I was happy that now there was nothing more to indicate that that crime had taken place here, at least on the outside. But on the inside, the wounds were still there.

*

To this day I am still undecided whether and even how I should wake the house from its deep slumber. In an interview several years ago I said once that I would perhaps demolish the house one day with explosives. That would at least make room for something new, something good to be created in its place.

It is difficult to find a solution for the house that makes sense. In the last several years I have tried to make it available for various charitable purposes, but its ominous past hangs over it. Who could imagine setting up a preschool there, or making it a residence for refugees? Even if you could forget the history of that place, something that the house itself cannot help, for one moment, there would still be innumerable statutory provisions that would make repurposing difficult. I still have not given up hope that someday the house can become something that will benefit others, whatever shape that may take.

140

# 8

# "A Matter of Decency"

## My Involvement in Sri Lanka

During my captivity I so desperately wished for help –
and it never came. I know how it feels to need help, and
in the end to have to depend on only yourself. That's
why standing up for others with the means available to
me was and still remains a matter close to my heart.

I had the desire to help even as a child. Sometimes I stole a few small
coins from the jar my mother kept in her shop for making change and
gave them to homeless people or beggars who hung around the "Renn-
bahnsiedlung", our council housing plan. My heart hammering in my
chest and gripping the coins tightly in my hand I would march up to
them and say, "This is for you. Please don't drink it away." Often enough
I would then see them at the kiosk with a handful of Austrian schillings,
enough for a beer or some liquor. I did not like it, and even today I still
have my problems with it. Maybe because as a child I saw too many
people who had lost part of their lives to alcohol. They had little pur-

pose in life, no job, no goals, and their daily existence was so marked by hopelessness and frustration that they would try to numb or drown it in alcohol.

My greatest hero was Don Bosco. His real name was Giovanni (John) Melchiorre Bosco, a Catholic priest and missionary who lived in the 19th century and was canonized as a saint in 1934. In 1859 he founded the Salesians of Don Bosco, and in 1872 he established the sister order Salesian Sisters of Saint John Bosco, also known as the Daughters of Mary Help of Christians. I heard about him and his work for the first time in religion class and immediately decided to follow in his footsteps to become a priest. But that is unfortunately a position reserved only for men still today, at least in the Catholic Church.

It is possible that I was so fascinated by him and his very special educational approach because in a way I saw myself reflected in the children he worked with. Children who were caught between worlds. Only allowed to be a child for short time, having to take on responsibility early in life or never loved enough. I myself did not have an intact environment in the way of a happy family consisting of a dad, a mom and a child, but I had a loving family. Both of my parents gave me the feeling that I was loved, that their failure at times was more due to circumstances, their lack of ability to cope with their separation that was felt in all areas of their daily lives.

In our neighbourhood at Rennbahnweg there were innumerable examples of "failed" families. Mothers who screamed at their children down in the courtyard, pushing them to the ground and beating them cruelly. Men who would literally beat their wives up and then boast at the kiosk while drinking liquor with their buddies that they showed their "old lady" who was boss once again. You could see those women skulking around the supermarket aisles having tried to carefully conceal their bruises with makeup. Older boys would lounge around the corridors leading to the individual housing blocks, molesting people as they walked by, and demanding money as a "toll" for being allowed to pass through. When I walked across the courtyards and the stairwells with my mother, she would always grab my hand a bit tighter. She tried to protect me as well as she could, and explain to me why she did not want me to play downstairs in the sandbox, and why she thought some of our neighbours were vulgar. Although her chief guiding motto in life was "Help yourself, because nobody else is going to do it", she made clear to me that there was something like a chain of causality. Those who had never experienced love and security, but a great deal of violence instead, would be very likely to repeat those behaviours with others.

While being held captive I asked myself repeatedly later on what the kidnapper must have experienced, what he was lacking, that made him capable of committing such a crime. That he could believe that his crime was the solution to his problems. A loser in the real world, who drew his strength from oppressing a child. An unstable person seeking the recognition that he probably did not receive enough of earlier in life. A man who possibly suffered a great deal under the dominance of his parents, but who in reality was never able to break free from them and was now trying to violently re-create this dynamic in his cellar world by reversing the roles. However, in the end this is just speculation. Even if it were true, it would naturally absolve him of nothing. At best it is merely an attempt to explain what is essentially unexplainable.

According to St. John Bosco, the raising and educating of children, either by parents or institutions, should be marked by genuine human kindness, supported by reason and rooted in faith. His actions were guided by the motto "I much prefer broken windows to broken hearts". A large poster of him hung on the outside of the door to my room. It was a portrait depicting him in warm, dark colours. As if I had wanted to signal to anyone about to come in my room that he was watching over me, that he kept an eye on me. While in captivity I tried to draw his face with his kind eyes from memory. Beneath the picture I wrote, "The power of evil draws its life from the cowardice of the good".

143

*

"A person does not have to be rich in order to give." That is also a quote from St. John Bosco. You have to want to help. After my escape that's exactly what I wanted to do. In my first interview I was asked how I planned to deal with the media's enormous interest in me, and whether or not it wasn't a bit too much to take:

*A bit too much? Well, yes. But on the other hand it has become clear to me that my fame (...) has given me a certain responsibility that I would also like to use. It has become clear to me (...) that you should use it (...) to benefit many people who can be helped. So I'm planning to set up a foundation, and I would like to carry out a number of aid projects that deal with issues like persons who have disappeared never to be found, like myself. There are also the kidnapped, abused and tortured and murdered young women for example who have gone missing in Mexico (...) and have been abused in the most brutal way. Furthermore, I am planning to set up a programme enabling people to help themselves in their fight against hunger, because I know how humiliating it is to let people go hungry.*

Looking back, it was perhaps too early, indeed just two weeks after my escape, to be talking about such issues. I underestimated just how much of an impact all of the tumult would have on me, how much time I would need to find my footing again in my new life in freedom. First I had to help myself and regain the necessary stability, which gave me the inner strength to advocate for others.

In the meantime I have supported a number of individuals, in South America but also in Austria. I have donated when a serious natural disaster has taken place somewhere in the world. Just like many others who

144

see the images of misery and suffering on the news, something like that is very moving to me. The violent forces of nature are in their own way very different than the violence exacted by humans. It triggers primeval fears and is something that we are unable to counter.

At Christmas in 2004 I saw pictures on TV that I was unable to process for a long time. People who were fleeing from floodwaters in panic, climbing onto rooftops and trees. People who were swept away by the foaming maelstrom, crushed between falling walls, floating cars and wooden beams. An earthquake in the Indian Ocean had triggered a devastating tsunami that struck the coastal areas of the surrounding countries. Over 230,000 died and over 1.7 million were homeless as a result. Nobody knew what was happening as the ocean slowly withdrew. A number of locals collected fish and mussels while tourists filmed the strange spectacle, commenting on what had just taken place with wonder and fascination. And then when the ocean returned again all at once, their voices becoming increasingly shrill and deafening. I sat transfixed in front of the small television in my dungeon. The terrible images and sounds haunted me for days. The picture that I painted at the time is still hanging in my apartment today.

Years later in 2007 I met a man at a birthday party who impressed me very much. Upali Sirimalwatta had been living in Vienna for 31 years and was working at the United Nations. After the tsunami hit he went on sabbatical for six months in order to establish an aid organization for his home country Sri Lanka. Since then he has returned again and again. He told me about the island in the Indian Ocean and about its fascinatingly beautiful natural landscape that contrasts so strikingly to the still very difficult political and economic situation in the country.

This small, thin man with warm eyes had a very special kind of energy and spoke to me with such an enthusiasm of his project in Sri Lanka that I definitely wanted to see him again. We made arrangements for additional meetings where he showed me pictures and told me about his work there. Now in retirement he was spending the majority of the year in Sri Lanka. He told me that it was not just the terrible tsunami, but also the civil war raging from 1983 to 2009 in the northern part of the country between the Tamil separatists and the Singhalese majority, who dominate the remainder of the country, a war with extremely serious consequences even today. Hundreds and thousands had lost their homes, and there were innumerable victims of torture and abuse, he told me.

In areas that are less developed for tourism grinding poverty is prevalent even today. There is very little infrastructure, and healthcare provision is rudimentary. Mothers and children bear the main brunt of the situation. The few outpatient clinics and hospitals had very few beds, if any at all, and they primarily took in only children. In Sri Lanka mothers would never allow themselves to be separated from their children if they had not reached a certain age. The precarious situation in the hospitals meant that they preferred to stay at home with their sick children so that they would not have to leave them alone in the hospitals. This is part of the reason that child mortality was so incredibly high in a number of regions.

I had absolutely no idea how desperate the situation was and how catastrophic the hygienic conditions really were until he showed me a number of pictures and videos taken during his most recent visit. The photographs and video clips showed a small decrepit building with crumbling plaster, and out in front a long line of people. The elderly, mothers with children, the sick. The interior images showed a large room with prominent mould stains everywhere. In between there were a couple of rusty metal beds that had once been painted white long ago. In an adjacent shed a couple of women were working on the ground next to an open fire. Above the burning wood was a steaming pot with an unidentified kind of food. This was the hospital kitchen, Upali informed me.

Hospital? I asked him where the medical equipment and the treatment rooms were. Or at least rooms that were worthy of those descriptions. He thumbed through the photographs and put some on the table in front of me. And antediluvian blood pressure measuring device, some bandages, a stethoscope, and oxygen tank, a couple of dark glass jars with dried roots or herbs. The worst was the delivery room. No European woman would want to give birth to her child there.

The hospital had an enormous catchment area. Most of the people who came here were rice farmers and manual labourers who worked on the large tea and rubber plantations. I tried to listen to what Upali was saying, but my eyes were drawn again and again to the photographs. I wondered how people living in such an environment were supposed to recover their health. When he told me that due to the limited amount of space new mothers were shown the door or separated from their babies even after high risk births, I made up my mind. I wanted to become active in Sri Lanka. Because the situation faced by the infants, toddlers and their mothers touched me I wanted to provide the appropriate funding so that a hospital ward could be set up especially for them. In Bulathsinghala in the Kalutara district, just adjacent to the old building that I had seen in Upali's photographs.

Because it's important not to offer help "from on high" by quickly sending an injection of funding from abroad that could disappear somewhere down the dark channels of corrupt bureaucracy, I asked Upali for help. He had connections and knew how the local authorities worked, what the local population needed and how to involve them. The aim was to respectfully share, not to patronize. In the end we decided to build a new hospital building with 25 inpatient beds, a building that could provide outpatient healthcare to up to 50,000 people a year. Upali would be on-site in Bulathsinghala, coordinating the construction work with an architect and report back to me on a regular basis. It was my wish that every cent would be used to benefit the local population and that the entire project could have a positive long-term effect on the area. The brick making machine purchased at the time for the project is still in operation. Many locals have found a job there, initially on the construction sites, and later in the hospital. In the meantime, a new housing development has even grown up around the hospital area.

After about a year of construction the building was ready. On 9 October 2011 I boarded the plane from Vienna to Colombo at around 11 PM to travel 7,450 km, with one stopover in Dubai, my longest trip to date. I was excited, and also a bit unsure of what I could expect there. What would the climate be like? With mosquitoes really as terrible as everyone said? How would I handle the packed itinerary and all of the meetings? Could I handle the strong sun, meeting so many strange people from a strange culture? I still have the utmost respect when meeting people who had suffered a fate that we fortunately could no longer imagine ever since Europe has been at peace.

In addition to the ceremonial inauguration of the Natascha Kampusch Children's Ward in Bulathsinghala, we were also planning to travel to northern Sri Lanka, to the area where the civil war had been fought. Together with a group of young people from the Austrian youth organization "Jugend Eine Welt – Don Bosco Aktion Österreich" I first wanted to visit a facility for victims of abuse in Uswetakeiyawa. The Bosco Sevana home housed around 80 boys between the ages of 11 and 19 who had been sexually abused "in the name of love". They had worked as so-called "beach boys", selling their bodies to paedophile sex tourists.

After another stopover north of Colombo at the Don Bosco Technical Centre, a school and training centre for orphans and underprivileged children, we were to head north to the formerly autonomous Tamil region. A home in Vavuniya provided refuge and professional medical care to girls, some who were former child soldiers and some who were war orphans, aged 10 to 24 years. Over half of them were war invalids, injured by grenade shrapnel and mines, making them dependent on regular medical care. Much more serious, however, were their psychological injuries. The traumatic experience of war, violence and abuse had impacted them for their entire lives. They were forced to watch as their parents and relatives were killed and/or lost their homes, and some of them were forced to fight in the guerrilla war on the side of the Tamil separatists. Fear, apathy and depression had become a constant companion for many of these children and adolescents. Many of them had been kidnapped or left behind when their families fled in panic, or remained as the only survivors after an attack. Not all of them viewed the end of the civil war as liberation. A feeling of renewed loss was mixed in with their happiness. Chiefly, it was a loss of their family and their close environment, then the loss of their rebel units or the violent military leader who decided whether they lived or died. Now they were faced with nothing.

I knew that meeting these women and girls would be an experience that would absolutely push me to my limits in many respects. I did not know what would be like to be confronted with what they had experienced. There were parallels, although the circumstances were completely different. There were wounds that could be seen, and wounds that festered beneath the surface. It was like confronting a nightmare. Up to 7,000 children and adolescents are said to have been deployed as fighters and coerced into killing during the civil war in Sri Lanka that lasted over 20 years. A lost generation.

\*

First of all I had to grapple with other concerns. Everybody had told me that when the door to the ice cold arrivals hall of the Bandaranaike International Airport opened, it would be like crashing into a wall of hot air and unbelievable humidity, as if somebody were throwing a bucket of water on you. I was surprised that I found the climate rather pleasant, a kind of gentle indoor swimming pool feel on my skin. So I was able to cross off number one on my list of concerns. Number two, mosquitoes and possibly malaria, was crossed off in the minibus that was already waiting for us. The mosquitoes were not so terrible that time of year, said the driver grinning broadly.

Colombo itself was an enormous teaming mass. Everywhere there were swarms of noisy people, and traffic on the streets proceeded but slowly and rather recklessly forward. Two-lane strips of asphalt were used to accommodate four lanes of traffic; three wheeled tuk tuks and mopeds weaved their way between colourfully painted and overloaded trucks. In the midst of all this were women with parasols and men wearing chequered sarongs. Now and again I was able to catch a glimpse of old, grand colonial buildings between the tall modern structures, as well as small canals full of garbage, along which the city's poor were housed in barracks.

It felt like an eternity until we left the city behind us, driving a ways along the coastline to the south. The wounds that the ocean had ripped open in December 2004 were still far from healed. All along the old coastal road you could still see – over seven years later – traces of devastation. Gaping holes where palm trees once stood in dense clusters. The skeletons of wrecked boats that now served as a photographic backdrop for tourists on the beaches. Mountains of debris where stray dogs were looking for something to eat. People who lived in partially collapsed ruins, many of them without work. After the catastrophe the government had decreed that the fisherman were no longer allowed to build their huts on the beach. For safety reasons, so they said. Funded by donations and land allocations, they were able to acquire small pieces of property in the interior of the country. But very few fishermen decided to become farmers. Moreover, the available slivers of beach have long been acquired in the meantime. By rich investors from abroad who now build spa oases for stressed out tourists.

The wounds inflicted on the population back then have also yet to heal. Many lost family members, and innumerable children have grown up without parents. There is hardly a family along the strip of coastline between Colombo and the former colonial centre of Galle in the South that has been spared. After spending the night in a hotel in Bentota we continued on to Uswetakeiyawa, to the Don Bosco home where padres were trying to give beach boys and other uprooted young men a new home and either an education or vocational training. Officially the institution was called a rehabilitation centre for former child prostitutes and children in high risk situations. After a number of welcoming speeches and a tour of the home, we went to the beach with a number of the boys. They showed us how they played cricket, using driftwood as bats, and talked me into playing football with them. I certainly was a not the most skilful football player in the world, but we all had fun and were served "coconut cocktails" afterwards: coconuts they collected themselves from the palm trees in the courtyard with a hole drilled in them and a straw.

The next day we drove to see Upali who welcomed us with refreshments on the patio of his house in the shade of mango and papaya trees. Even on the way to his house I was completely enchanted by the scenery. Everything was green; I had never seen such vegetation before in my life. Tea and rubber plantations, rice paddies with water buffalo and white herons continually taking flight. It may sound strange, but this landscape was so perfect that it was difficult to square it with what had happened to the people in that country.

One look at the clock told us that it was high time to be on our way again. Out on the patio we once again went through every detail. Upali had prepared me for the fact that the opening of the Children's Hospital would be such an enormous event. Local politicians would be on hand, even the minister of health. It was to be broadcast live on television, and the entire location was decorated with colourful tiny flags. There was even a parade with music, folkloric dancing with men in traditional costumes, wearing white sarongs and red hats with pom-poms and silver decorations.

My tension mounted on our way to the event; however, I felt more happy than overwhelmed. After a number of welcoming ceremonies the entire retinue proceeded to the square in front of the hospital. They had placed a lectern with a microphone in front of several rows of chairs that were by far not enough. There were 300 to 400 people there, as the minister proudly informed me.

During his speech I sat in the place of honour, but I had difficulty concentrating. Again and again I felt somebody touching my arm or my head timidly, followed by an apology and a question as to whether the colour of my hair was real, "So light…" I certainly stood out.

Then it was my turn. I was certainly a little bit nervous, as I was to speak in English. In conclusion I said, "During my captivity I said to myself, if I managed to escape one day, I will try to make this world a better place. I needed time to find my place in freedom. But now I feel that I'm strong enough to help others. I wish you all every success and the best of health."

Afterwards we proceeded to the ceremonial opening. The minister was a bit childish and insisted on cutting the blue ribbon in front of the entrance first. Somebody handed us a tray with two pairs of scissors, one pink, one light blue. Because the minister was in such a hurry, we got in each other's way a bit, so that in the end he ended up with the pink pair of scissors. Afterwards we were both supposed to light a kind of small paper tree with a candle. My tree did not want to catch a light, something that obviously amused him. In any case, we had a good laugh later on in the bus. I placed the last brick in the wall, then the tour of the building began. The thought that the rooms would be full of life in the next several days, that here doctors and nurses would be able to successfully treat a large number of mothers and children here made me very happy. During my abduction I often imagined to myself what it would be like if I were to break a bone or to contract sepsis. It is horrific to know that you would not receive any help.

Back in Vienna, I was asked by a journalist whether I suffered from a kind of "do-gooder syndrome". I found it strange, because after all we are also familiar with the concept of "decency". Ethics tell us that we need to do what is necessary. And if I have the means, i.e. see it as correct and an important duty to make an attempt to help. The hospital cost € 50,000, roughly equivalent to one euro per person who can be treated in the hospital in one year. This is a tiny amount of money; back in Vienna, even a small cup of coffee in a café costs more.

For me the greatest gift is that the hospital was accepted by the local population from the date it was opened. Sometimes I receive letters and photographs sent to me by children who have their picture taken in front of the commemorative plaque and the picture of the "donor". It is moving, but also a bit uncomfortable. After all I primarily paid forward the donations that other people had given me so many years before.

*

Early next day we set off, as the trip up north was to take over six hours. There was no highway yet and traffic on the small, in some cases unpaved roads was hellish. We arrived in Vavuniya completely exhausted.

The sisters running the home received us very warmly. We enjoyed a meal together at a long wooden table. The food was served on large banana leaves, and we ate it with our fingers. The younger children at the table had a good laugh at me, because I kept dribbling pieces of rice, and after a short time my dress already had a few stains. But fortunately it had a colourful flowered pattern so that the stains were not all that prominent. After our meal I was surrounded by young girls who insisted on braiding my hair, putting makeup on me and dancing with me. It was so wonderful to see how free and relaxed they were, so in the moment and so natural with me.

For the first time in my trip I had come to a place where my past played absolutely no part. Because simply nobody had heard about it. I was one of several young people in a group expressing interest and a desire to get involved. Everybody approached the others with an open mind, because nobody knew anything about the other person's past. It wasn't until I began talking with the sisters and the older girls that I began to slowly reveal snippets of my story. The mother superior asked

153

a number of follow-up questions, because she could not understand the meaning of my kidnapping. How anybody could come up with the idea of imprisoning somebody else for so many years just like that. The children that she was working with had had clear responsibilities from the point of view of their kidnappers. The rebels used them to spread fear and horror, to subjugate entire villages, saying that if they did not cooperate they had the ways and means to achieve their goal. But without the backdrop of war and terror, so to speak without being faced with a "dire situation", throwing somebody on her way to school into a car and locking her up was something that she just could not comprehend. It wasn't until I told her, "Sometimes I thought he simply wanted to have a slave," that she was silent for a long time, taking my hands in hers nodding. That one sentence was enough for her. She did not need to know more.

I found Nitiya's story particularly moving. She has come to the home at the age of 18 two years before my visit. It wasn't until a year later that she began to talk. Until then she had neither spoken nor laughed once; she had even refused to put down her weapon. She had been kidnapped at the age of four, her entire family had been killed, her village burned down. The children who were unable to flee were abducted. She was forced to address the rebel leader of her unit as "God" and "Father". Anyone refusing to do so was abused and raped. In her first several years she was to collect the dead bodies, then later she was told to kill people herself. Each of them had worn an explosive belt on their bodies in order to detonate themselves if they came in contact with the enemy so as to take a couple of other people with them when they died. After she fled she wandered around the conflict area for months until the international Red Cross brought her to the Don Bosco sisters.

I found my encounters with Nitiya, as well as with other people on my trip, extremely enriching. Because on one hand we approached each other very openly, but on the other hand we kept our distance in order to show respect. Not always discussing the full horror of one's experiences is sometimes done out of protection. Not protecting oneself, but protecting others. In the past I have had experiences that confused me at first and left me puzzled. On one hand enormous interest, sympathy even, and on the other hand the constant pressure to reveal additional details. This never wanting to stop, this inability to let it be, as if to say, there must be even more to be uncovered. And at the same time this pushing it back into the private realm – that's where it belongs, if at all – whenever I have spoken openly about my trauma. Whenever somebody told me, "I didn't want to know that," I felt rejected. It was painful, but I have learned in the meantime that this is a protective mechanism, a fear of being overwhelmed, of an inability to cope.

For me both of these scenarios are very difficult to deal with, but I have gotten better at it. The compartmentalization as well as the reduction of this one phase of my life are both mechanisms that I cannot understand. I only have this one life. I only have this one image of myself – even though I am able to view it from a different angle thanks to my additional life experience. On the outside my life can certainly be broken down into various phases. Into a before, a during, and an after. Nevertheless those phases cannot be separated from each other. Because everything impacts everything else, and for me one is inconceivable without the other.

It is not necessary to examine such extreme experiences as mine or those that I encountered in Sri Lanka, under the microscope. We all know that horrific things happen on this planet, everywhere, every day, every second. Enormous catastrophes or terrible events that happen to only one person shake us. For a moment we are shocked, express compassion or donate money. But often we only register such events if they cross a certain line, in terms of their scope or our ability to imagine them. And that's where we start to measure, to compare, to put suffering in context.

I don't know if it is a matter of faith, but the sisters and priests in the two homes I visited simply accepted their charges the way they were. They did not make acceptance and empathy contingent on the severity of their experiences, but simply on the fact that a person was standing in front of them who needed help and protection.

I felt a connection with the children and young adults that I met in Sri Lanka, as if we were bound together by a magical link. Despite the terrible circumstances my story has had a positive ending. And the stories of these children have also had a positive ending. They now have clean beds to sleep in and sanitary facilities with water they are even able to drink. They are provided with medical and psychological care, they are receiving an education, an opportunity to restart their lives. While the images of their old lives will never fully disappear, they will fade over time. They can experience moments of happiness and receive support from people who have a clear conscience. When we said goodbye, Nitiya showed me her room. In the drawer of her small dresser there was a picture of Don Bosco.

9

# On a Continuous Loop

## *"Natascha-Gate"*

Today ten years after my escape I have no tolerance for
the fact that there are many people who believe that
they must make a name for themselves at my expense,
by reinterpreting and twisting the facts as it suits them,
thereby victimizing my family and myself a second
time. Making us a victim of their inability to accept the
crime as such, just as it was.

In the above-mentioned interview on my trip to Sri Lanka I was asked
whether I was happy:

You're always asking questions. What is happiness? Happiness is
ephemeral. There are perhaps brief moments where you are at peace
with the world. Here in Sri Lanka I have been fortunate to experience a large number of these kinds of moments over the last several
days. I am blossoming here like a cactus that suddenly sprouts small

pink blooms. Like a beautiful, large orchid.

*What is different in Vienna?*

In Vienna I am often attacked. I have to be on alert all the time. An invisible set of rules surrounds me and constrains me, oppressing me at the same time. Here in Sri Lanka I feel safer. I think that after this experience I will be able to breathe much easier in Vienna. It's as if an enormous burden has been taken from me.*

I felt as if I were headed in the right direction and had found meaning for myself. I had hardly returned to Vienna when a number of people began to gripe that there were enough children in Austria who are suffering, and on top of all that I certainly could have invested even more money. Elsewhere I have already mentioned that very few people appreciate it when others attempt to poke around in their financial dealings. Apparently many people seem to suffer from the misconception that I am doing quite well in terms of my personal wealth. Far be it from me to feel the need to justify myself or anything, but maybe knowing this will silence a number of critics. I have never spent a single cent of the donations I have received on myself. I have supported projects with disabled children in Austria, earmarked € 25,000 in immediate assistance for the Fritzl family and called on the Austrian people to donate to the victims of this horrific crime. A number of media outlets and blogs never attribute honest compassion to me. No, they accused me of "patronizing behaviour". An additional € 25,000 has been earmarked for the hospital in Sri Lanka, where I matched that amount from my own pocket.

After my first interview a journalist wrote, "It is also very clever, just on a side note, that she is making money off of her story. Anyone having

---

* Kronenzeitung, 16. Oktober 2011, http://www.krone.at/Oesterreich/Kampusch_Ich_wollte_schon_immer_anderen_helfen-Einsatz_in_Sri_Lanka-Story-299552 (Version: August 2016)

to come to terms with such a horrific tale should, like her, not have to be concerned about money. And if the world is so intensely interested in her fate, then it should be willing to pay money for it."*

To those for whom this is once again grist for their mill I would like to say: I genuinely feel sorry for those who think that I am doing so unbelievably well, that they would change places with me in a heartbeat. They really should make an honest effort to put themselves in my shoes for once. They should try to spend a day or even a week in such a confined space. They should take a look at my life today, hounded by conspiracy theorists trying to make themselves look important and unable to let go. Again and again called before court or to speak into a microphone in order to testify to the whole story again and take a position on the most absurd accusations. In the meantime it seemed to me as if all of Austria was full of people, all the way up to the highest levels, who, figuratively speaking, were out and about with microwave ovens and gas stoves looking to reheat my story again and again. Yes, I would really like to see these people spend an entire day in my shoes.

\*

How did one press expert put it so concisely in August 2006: "In four weeks the story will have run its course journalistically speaking and will be out of the media." To this very day the story is still stuck in the media. It is not easy even for me to keep track of all of the developments, all the twists and turns that my story has taken.** For me, the issue actually ended with my escape and the death of the kidnapper. A clear case that should be open and shut, which had run its course legally speaking

---

\* Die Welt, 21 December 2006
\*\* See also the Chronology of Events in the Appendix

around two months after my escape when the investigation was closed.

However, like during my captivity, the police and the public prosecutors have been pressured to continue their investigation. Because, it was said, there was a pornography ring involving the highest circles of power, because I was being blackmailed with incriminating evidence and for that reason was attempting to impede the full clarification of the case, etc. Statements from the public prosecutors that there was no basis for these speculations fell on deaf ears; the conspiracies continued to run wild.

Parallel to this there were indications that errors in the investigation could have been made, that there had possibly been a cover up, supposedly so as not to endanger the upcoming general elections by making such a scandal public. The Ministry of the Interior responded and set up an evaluation commission in February 2008. One month later a parliamentary fact-finding committee was formed in order to shed light on the internal processes.

I was of the opinion that if there could actually have been errors, and as a consequence cover ups, then that should be comprehensively cleared up so that the competent authorities could draw their conclusions. The thought that it might have been possible to find me much sooner was painful, but it serves no purpose to cling to hypotheticals, like "could've, should've, would've". That kind of thinking will only eat you up.

As events wore on, my underlying positive attitude began to show significant cracks, and my trust in the system was significantly shaken. When I said as much, as I have often done openly, in a statement, it was not particularly well received. I was forced to publicly apologize – this was not only difficult to understand looking back, if you consider everything that had happened: Excerpts from police interviews provided to the commission and the fact-finding committee suddenly appeared completely out of context and in an abridged version in the press. Although the members of the commission and the committee had signed agreements to maintain confidentiality. The passages that were published had nothing to do with the actual task at hand (namely clarifying possible internal failures), but became an opportunity to discredit me, and later my family as well.

I was accused of participating in a cover up in order to prevent the unearthing of a much larger crime. For my parents this must have seemed like a nightmarish déjà vu. Everything had resurfaced. The accusations of abuse, the possible connections to the kidnapper, or rather an entire group of kidnappers, the "environment" that I likely came from and had given me such terrible childhood experiences, as asserted by Ludwig Adamovich, the head of the evaluation commission. There was no tangible evidence, but it was something you had to "just sense. However, the fact that Mr. Priklopil was out and about one fine day with his delivery van and had looked to see if some girl was walking along that he could make use of is something I find absurd."* When highly respected people like him – himself the former president of the Austrian Constitutional Court – spread such ideas (and those weren't the only ones), everyone feels safe in saying, "Well, if that's the way he sees it, there must be something more there."

Both Adamovich as well as commission member Johann Rzeszut, former president of the Supreme Court, were both in agreement that there was possibly a little bit more to it than the official version of my story. In a published letter to the Austrian daily Österreich Rzeszut wrote that it was completely unrealistic that an individual criminal would concoct a plan to kidnap a child using a car all by himself. And if I should ever decide one day to "go public and expose the full truth in the media" I would be in danger for my life, as possible masterminds "may just decide that they are forced to take action and put an end to things." He said that for years he feared nothing more than "a newspaper article stating that 'Natascha Kampusch was found dead'". From the perspective of the victim "a host of possible motivations for the conscious decision to pro-

---

* Profil, 29th edition, 13 July 2009

vide false information was conceivable: an ever closer relationship with the kidnapper over a long period, ongoing pressure brought to bear by a criminal not yet identified by police, cover-up of the involvement of persons close to her, etc."*

If his concern for my life was so great, the immediate question is why I was to learn of this apparently acutely dangerous situation from the media. That was certainly not in the interest of my safety, but apparently served the needs of a number of committee members for recognition and affirmation.**

The responses that I was subject to from public were reflected in the status of each of the "new investigations". From October 2008 to January 2010 the case was reopened once again. The final findings, from my point of view clear from the very beginning, were that Priklopil had acted alone. There was no connection to any masterminds, not to mention my parents.

During this period I was forced again and again to look backwards into my past. I was unable to have any kind of future if the past was stuck to the soles of my feet like a clump of manure. Not because I wouldn't have been able to cope with it, but because I was once again pushed into that pile of manure. By people who believed to have found a forum to achieve maximum attention.

So as not to be misunderstood: I would have been the first to welcome genuinely new approaches. I would have never done anything to impede any further clarification of the case, if there had been anything to clear up. From the first to my last police interview I constantly reiterated, mantra-like, what I knew. And that dovetailed exactly with what various evaluation commissions and fact-finding committees have "unearthed" in the meantime.

In 2009 I was required to appear in court in Graz several times with-

---

* Österreich, 10 August 2009
** See also: Kommission agiert "unverantwortlich", Der Standard, 10 August 2009

in the framework of new investigations. The questioning took place behind closed doors; but in front of the courthouse curious onlookers and camera teams were jockeying for position. One of the reporters was so keen that he fell into a flowerpot. Over the next several days I was smuggled into the building through the cellar. Two public prosecutors grilled me, once for an entire eight hours, asking me questions again and again about particular sequences of events. Why I did not run away earlier, whether statement X came from such and such person, when I was questioned where and by whom, and what I said during those questionings. It was fatiguing and very trying for me both physically and mentally. Although the window was open, the air was incredibly stuffy. Very quickly my head began to hurt and I had difficulty concentrating.

Later my statements were compared to the official police reports of my initial interviews. They were no deviations, meaning that I had stuck to my statements, stuck to the truth. Nevertheless it seemed as if all of a sudden nearly everything concerning my person and my story was branded a lie by certain circles. In January 2010 for example, the Austrian news magazine Profil reported that I had escaped twice during my captivity, but had returned to my captor twice "voluntarily". The magazine quoted an investigator from the commission saying, "The intention is to uphold the image of eight years in chains. But that's not how it was."* I was outraged and saw the report as a low point in the reporting on my past. It was not to be the last.

The entire years-long "Kampusch case" was essentially a farcical waste of tax revenue and resources. The 600-page final report issued by the Innsbruck public prosecutor's office alone, which had spent ten months focusing on the internal processes of the Vienna public prosecutor's office, can essentially be reduced to one sentence: Nobody hastily zeroed in on Priklopil as the sole kidnapper; there is simply no indication that he was not acting alone. This was in November 2011. But, there's a saying

---

* Profil, 3 January 2010

in German that what is not permitted to be true, cannot be true. And so it goes, again and again.

*

In my hometown of Vienna, which is both a big city and a village, being a "public person" means nothing more than having to answer questions publicly. The Viennese are well-informed and make no secret of that fact. During the phase of the legal, and also political, tug-of-war, during the phase of the media overheating over "Natascha-Gate", every step I took was like running the gauntlet. Whenever I took public transportation, various camps emerged depending on their curiosity, empathy or hate levels. Some approached me with their sympathy – Will it never end? What are they doing to you? - While others said that they had already known all along, while still others asked me obscene questions of what it was like to have been "always at his beck and call" and what kind of contraception we used.

Groups of teenage boys were particularly intrusive. Whenever I refused to respond to their comments, they would begin to yell insults or bellow obscene jokes. "Where does the biggest bush grow? In the cellar, in the cellar!" Or: "All the kids play with Playmobil, but Natascha plays with Priklopil."

Psychologists say that people always use humour to process the incomprehensible. The blacker and more macabre the joke is, the more it meets its purpose of putting difficult to comprehend horrors into words and coping with it in the face of our helplessness. Once I had managed to escape from my abductor, it only took a few days for the first Kampusch jokes to make their rounds in Austria. In principle I have no problem with that. I'm actually a very fun-loving person. I like to laugh, and I am certainly more than able to laugh at myself. But standing in a crowded tram, gripping the handrail tightly or wanting to disappear into my seat, while everybody around me is bellowing and roaring is humiliating. In situations like that I have often dashed off the tram at the next station, the howls echoing behind me, and people staring scornful daggers at my back. It's something else entirely if you are sitting with friends and after a couple glasses of wine you trot out your best jokes, as opposed to seeking to expose a person in public who has become the victim of a crime through no fault of their own.

If these instances of atrocious behaviour were only committed by teenagers, I could say "Forget about it. It's just a stupid phase. All they want is to assert their independence and get attention while protected by a group of people." But the atrocious behaviour that adults have displayed toward me has been incomparably worse. They always occurred when the media had once again reported on supposedly new revelations, a new scandal in the "Kampusch case".

When suspicions cropped up in the media that I had given birth to a baby while in captivity, and the baby had been buried either dead or alive, depending on which version you read, the behaviour became particularly bad. The rumour first started in April 2008 during the piecemeal publication of confidential dossiers. Now, at the end of 2011, when everything appeared to be over, the rumour resurfaced. A number of the politicians from the far-right Austrian Freedom Party (FPÖ) opined that "there were strong indications" that I might have given birth to a baby while in the kidnapper's dungeon. It was possible that it was buried in the garden, or was still living at an unknown location."*

Giving rise to these claims were a lock of hair and a small pamphlet on the anatomy and care of infants that the police had found among my belongings in the dungeon. The pamphlet was nothing more than something to read, just like my Julia novels, the encyclopaedias, the newspapers, comics or adventure and science fiction books that the kidnapper

---

* www.bz-berlin.de/artikel-archiv/natascha-kampusch-kind-mit-dem-entführer (Version:

brought to my dungeon. The lock of hair was mine. I had cut it off before the kidnapper shaved my head so that I could remember what my hair felt like and what colour it had had.

Although the investigating authority had fully examined the garden of the house in Strasshof with probes and had naturally failed to find the remains of a child, rumours that I was potentially a "baby murderer" faded but gradually. And although the examinations at the Vienna General Hospital unmistakably proved that I had never been pregnant at any time, the fact-finding committee in Parliament was to re-examine the issue. A number of publications put the story on their front page yet again. When I unsuspectingly left my flat early one morning while this was going on, an older woman rushed over to me and smacked me on the head with a rolled up newspaper saying, "Where did you bury that poor baby, you pig?!" After attacking me, she tossed the paper carelessly on the ground and stomped off. The headline on the cover page provided plenty of information as to which article the lady had apparently just finished reading.

On the Internet I was called a "whore". They said that what I really needed was "someone to really give it to me" because Priklopil, that uptight prude, had apparently not been up to the task. "She would certainly like that, that slut!" On the metro people would whisper behind me that I should be locked away so that the public would be spared from having to look at my face. I received letters, in which men spun pages-long fantasies about "obedient women" who they wanted to humiliate and treat with the utmost of contempt. These were attitudes that I had never experienced while in captivity in this way. And I had naïvely believed that I had been subject to the singularity of one single diseased mind.

On good days I was able to dismiss all of the humiliations. They didn't really mean me. They were seeking an outlet for their perverse fantasies. On bad days it frightened me so much that I simply hid myself

August 2016)

166

in my apartment. I did not answer the phone, did not open the door, no matter who was ringing the bell.

This contempt for women, the general lack of respect and propensity to violence toward others, coupled with a bizarre idea of (repressed) sexuality, the abuse fantasies and perhaps even terrible experiences of this kind are still a taboo subject in our society. Awareness for and attention to these issues has certainly grown in the wake of large-scale scandals that even the church has undergone in the last several years. But taking an important and clear eyed look at the overarching structures, as well as possible cover-up operations in the church and – as has been mentioned in my case – at so-called pornography rings potentially behind such crimes, as well as concentrating on the big picture equally and very conveniently distorts our view of the small picture. The everyday extremes in families in our immediate environment, in our neighbourhoods, in public. We train our gaze on them when curiosity drives us to, and we look away when we're afraid of being unable to cope with what we see there. However, the same wolf who devours the little lambs can also mingle among the flock undetected in sheep's clothing.

In my case it was clear who the real wolf was. Not to the outside world, not to the neighbourhood and his immediate environment. But to me. Over the course of my captivity he had gone from kidnapper to the only person I had a close relationship with, despite me never losing sight of his crime. He was the man who robbed me of my family, my childhood and adolescence. Over the years he became an opponent that I came to increasingly meet on equal footing as a result of the specific relationship between kidnapper and victim.

I was not on equal footing with the "wolves" that crossed my path after my escape. I couldn't be. They pretended to be rescuers, working toward uncovering the mysteries of the case, and were equipped with enormous power and reach. They instrumentalized and were instrumentalized themselves in turn. I was transformed from victim to a potential (co-)criminal, a liar.

And so it was that errors in the investigation that had given rise to actual questions were dealt with relatively swiftly and receded into the background. For example ignoring statements made by eyewitnesses, or tips such as the one provided by the canine police officer who knew of a strange man who seemed like someone who would commit such crime. A serious follow-up of that clue might possibly have changed my situation. Although even an inspection of the house and property with sniffer dogs just after my abduction would likely not have resulted in finding me. Access to my dungeon was too perfectly concealed, and the room built for me by the kidnapper was too far below ground and behind walls that were far too thick. His precautionary measures were too perfect, starting with the white delivery van filled with construction debris when the police questioned him in the scope of a large-scale search, including the shaving of my head and the removal of garbage from the house, which was not disposed of in his own garbage container, but in public garbage containers across a wide radius so that nobody could find traces of me.

What remained: A rumour mill that could not be backed up with any kind of evidence. When asked, the gentlemen responded evasively and even cryptically by pointing to their confidentiality obligations concerning ongoing investigations or by complaining that the investigation was being impeded. Because the whole truth was being covered up, and important documents and facts were being kept from them: once everything had finally come to light, "a number of people would end up losing face, first and foremost Natascha Kampusch herself". But achieving such a feat was not that easy, as Mr. Adamovich put it, "You try bringing down an icon!"*

That seemed to be what they were aiming at. Only: Why did my statements, why did the truth finally have to be refuted?

It was clear what was to be brought to light. "We mustn't forget one

---

* Profil, 29th edition, 13 July 2009

thing. It was an abduction without any demands for ransom, and there was no child custody dispute going on in the background. What do we have left? The sexual component. (…) It goes without saying that society not only has the right, but also an interest in such matters if a potential second paedophile is running around free. Particularly if there are a number of indications that (…) a paedophilia ring is possibly receiving a steady supply of material."[*]

How similar the statements are. That was three years after the open letter to the Austrian daily Österreich. In the meantime the case had been closed (January 2010), another parliamentary fact-finding committee had been formed (December 2011), and one month before the Rzeszut interview with News the rumour of the "Kampusch-Priklopil baby" had once again veered off in a bizarre direction. A police detective had appeared in a school in Laxenburg[**], ostensibly to educate the children on road safety. The teacher was struck speechless when he presented a photograph and asked for items with the DNA of the girl in the picture. When questioned by the school principal, he reported to have been hired to look for the daughter of Ms. Kampusch. The underlying suspicion was that I had given the baby to the sister of Priklopil's friend Ernst H., who raised the child. After the incident she filed a complaint with the police and actually had genetic testing done, which unambiguously demonstrated that she was the mother. Nobody spared any thought as to the impact of pursuing this conspiracy theory on the mother, the daughter or even her classmates.

Circumstantial evidence that the police detective may not have acted entirely on his own accord, but rather in connection with retired Supreme Court judge Rzeszut, were conclusively debated in court in early summer 2015. The matter at hand concerned accusations of false testimony. Initially Rzeszut had said that he did not know the detective

---

[*] Rzeszut in an interview with News, 5 March 2012
[**] A town in Lower Austria just south of Vienna.

at all, but later admitted that he had met him twice at a café, nothing more. An examination of telephone records painted an entirely different picture: several instances of contact prior and subsequent to the incident in Laxenburg. When questioned, he said that he might have had "a mental tunnel" and that given the "host of telephone calls" he was unable for the life of him "to remember every minor telephone call".

The judge was very understanding, "I believe that you should have the benefit of the doubt that you forgot to mention it." And moreover, "I am sorry that you have had to be subjected to this."*

*

It would've been nice for me to hear something similar at least once from somebody sitting in a similar position. Instead, the matter dragged on. In June 2012 the decision was made to completely reopen the "Kampusch case" once again, this time to reach out to outside specialists for help. Cold case experts from the FBI and the German Federal Criminal Office (BKA) were deployed, spending weeks sifting through thousands of files that first had to be translated for the American officials. Three quarters of a year later the experts confirmed that police had failed to follow up on a number of clues, that Priklopil had acted alone, that he had no connections to ominous pornography rings and that he had actually committed suicide.

After several years and innumerable detours the only thing left was what we had from the very beginning. There was a special broadcast on television where German criminal experts presented their findings. Political leaders and legal experts were also invited. When questioned on the cold case specialists' findings a politician from the far-right Austrian

---

* Kronenzeitung, 27 February 2015

170

Freedom Party (FPÖ) said, "I think that if Ms. Kampusch were to in fact feel the need one day to perhaps tell the whole truth - and it has been proven that she did not always tell the whole truth everywhere at times – this may naturally result in continued follow-up investigations."*

It would appear that nobody will ever allow the case to be closed. But arguments or truth are simply no defence against conspiracy theories. The insanity lives on.

---

* Dagmar Belakowitsch-Jenewein in the news broadcast ZIB, 15 April 2013

# *Epilogue*

25 years of my life and still
I'm trying to get up that great big hill of hope
For a destination
I realized quickly when I knew I should
That the world was made of this brotherhood of man
For whatever that means
(...)
And I try
Oh my god do I try
I try all the time
In this institution
(...)
And so I wake in the morning
And I step outside
And I take a deep breath and I get real high
And I scream from the top of my lungs
What's going on?*

A while ago I heard that song on the radio once again and it reminded

---

* Excerpt from the lyrics for What's Up? by 4 Non Blondes, which came out in 1992 on their debut album "Bigger, Better, Faster, More!"

me of how important it was for me and my cousin, with whom I spent a great deal of time with as a child. We almost ended up fighting about who liked the song more and who had heard it more often.

I've always been able to lose myself and then find myself again in music and in many a song text. During my captivity there were some days where I screamed the lines from the song "You don't own me. I'm not just one of your many toys. You don't own me" filling the space in my dungeon in an effort to bolster my morale. On other days I laid in a ball on my bed, only able to whimper, "Don't tell me what to do. Don't put me on display, don't try to change me, don't tie me down." That very same song also contains the words "I'm free and I love to be free, to live my life in the way I want".* Those lines gave me something to hold onto, and they were a promise for the future. Finally able to live my life, just as I had always imagined. In the last ten years that was the greatest gift that I have given myself: Freedom. The joy at having come through this difficult time gave me strength. I was so full of energy and drive, and wanted to do everything all at once, to make all of my dreams come true, if not in the next two minutes, then at least in the next two years. Even as a child I was highly driven to take control of my own life. And I often imagined what it would be like to be an adult. Then I would do something that would amaze everybody, and I would surpass even myself. As a child I lacked the self-confidence that I projected on my "adult ego" during captivity, that I would someday take myself by the hand and lead myself to freedom. In my thoughts I was always free, and ten years ago I actually succeeded in overcoming the walls of my captivity. My past impacts my life today inasmuch as it has naturally left its mark on me and given me a certain strength and ability to reflect. During my eight and a half years of captivity I learned to make the best of my situation, however impossible it may seem. I have tried not to repay evil with evil, to

---

* "You don't own me", originally sung by Lesley Gore; however, there is also a version sung by Bette Midler

avoid allowing myself to be destroyed by negative energies and to remain human. Even back then it helped me to keep up an inner dialogue with myself. First it was for lack of anybody else to talk to, then to satisfy a deeper need. I'm very aware of myself. I see myself and try to have a very clear overview of my inner workings. Sometimes I gaze directly into the abyss. That can be shocking, even with other people, but these kinds of depths are part of you. With the help of therapy, I am trying to cleanse my psyche, my mind and my soul and to question things. I'm trying to give my head and my gut the necessary space to navigate a balance between the two.

I have been able to gain valuable experience in the last ten years in freedom. Wonderful, but also very trying experiences. Sometimes I have woken up and asked myself what is actually "going on" in the song sung by the 4 Non Blondes. In some phases of my life I did not have the feeling that I had anything under control. The despair and powerlessness I have felt have in some cases done more to undermine me than the abuses that I was subjected to by the kidnapper.

The most difficult of these was coming to terms with my story and the reactions to it. Coming to terms with all of my perceptions of the world and the emotions that these have triggered in me and that I have triggered in others. Coming to terms with the expectations, hopes and disappointments. In these last several years I have sometimes felt like a wall, speckled and painted over with all sorts of paints and coverings, until in the end I was unrecognizable even to myself.

Most people I have met, either from my family or complete strangers, had a version of me in their heads. Everybody had different pictures that were projected on me. Either in an attempt to radically separate themselves from me and reject my kidnapping and my imprisonment by rejecting me. Or they saw themselves reflected in me in some way. This reflection is something that we do all the time, every day. It's part of how we coexist with others in society. While in captivity I had only to meet and reflect the needs of one single person. I managed to engage with him without losing track of myself. After my escape I was completely overwhelmed at having to meet the needs, expectations and attributions of a wide variety of people. I believed I had to meet them, I had to understand and accept what other people thought was right. What path they thought was right for me without being able to recognize where that would lead me. Now this sounds a bit abstract, but it's possible to picture it this way. One person tells you turn left, while the other says turn right, and a third person tells you that it's best not to go anywhere at all.

In the midst of all of this – in most cases well-intentioned – advice from others, there was a time where I lost myself a little bit. And I had sworn to myself that I would remain authentic. That was not all that easy, because I was caught between so many other people's interests and motives, pulling me in different directions and changing over time. In the last several years a wide variety of forces have tried to appropriate my story. Marlene Streeruwitz predicted back in 2006 that precisely this mechanism would come into play, shortly after my first interview:

*A failure to cope everywhere. A society shows itself in its ability to only express need or admiration. Envy and idealization must be added to the proffered story, thereby taking possession of it. The story as told undergoes a rewrite as soon as it is being told. In rejection or aversion. In this way, the story belongs to everybody. The listeners, while listening, take the place of the storyteller, filling the story with their own associations and connections. (...) Here we are completely exposed to this specific victim who is Natascha Kampusch (...), but each of us has a vague feeling of being a victim ourselves. (...) Assumptions are made. We project. The inability to think "victim" (...) [results in the fact that] being a victim is a condition that we prefer to keep secret so no counter-narrative is incited that robs the victim a second time.*"

---

* Marlene Streeruwitz: „Umstellt von Erziehern", Der Freitag, 15 September 2006

The experts analyzing my life have included journalists, who have filled in the gaps, who were looking to, or were expected to expand on my story to improve circulation figures; politicians seeking to burnish their image as someone who gets to the bottom of things; representatives of the judicial system and law enforcement, who have been positioned in opposition to each other; self-proclaimed unveilers of "the whole truth"; etc. Caught in the middle was the public that gradually no longer knew what to think. Of me, and the entire case, and over time preferred in their haste, so to speak, to meet me with rejection rather than understanding.

This was very difficult to take on an everyday basis. At the beginning I wondered every time what these people now thought of me, what they saw in me, what they know, what caused the coldness in their eyes.

I have spent – or have had to spend – a great deal of time, also in therapy, in accepting the idea that not everything that happens has directly to do with me as a person or my character. But rather that my story has slowly become unmoored from the reality as it actually took place and as I experienced it. How it has become gradually separate from my life and my lived reality. In the meantime I have made up my mind that many new developments and revelations and the reactions to them are no longer of interest to me. Must not be of any interest to me, otherwise it will end up running me down in the end. I do not have to drink every cup of hemlock that somebody hands me or even feel guilty when I push it away.

During my years of captivity I felt as if somebody had hollowed me out and stolen my life. In the last several years I sometimes felt as if my ability to be myself had been taken from me. Again and again I have been asked in interviews how I'm doing. Whether I am happy and finally truly free. Sometimes I would have loved to have said, no, otherwise I wouldn't be sitting here, and otherwise I wouldn't be heading for a new round of insults. The sad part about it is that these questions are often meant rhetorically. Very few people truly wanted to know that I am making an effort to go through life with a positive attitude. Despite everything, and particularly because of it. What law is there that says that when you have suffered or run into a rough patch once, that you have to remain trapped in a downward negative spiral until the end of your days?

It was one of the most upsetting experiences that I had in dealing with other people, that many people had this very particular attitude of being a prisoner of your destiny. I'm not allowed to be happy, because... That cannot be the case, because... People that only see the negative in themselves, never the positive, the strong, even when it has remained buried for a long time. Every person is an individual, and everybody's destiny is different. But I firmly believe that we are not just subject to the whims of fate. We can empower ourselves to accept the greatest gift that life gives us: The freedom to shape it.

I now feel that I am slowly able to live out the aspects of my personality that make me me: full of energy and drive with a strong will.

I know that in many ways I will not be able to shake the effects of the second part of my life. But for the future I hope that when I am in the process of swimming free, others do not try to block my path. I was not allowed to spend my entire adolescence the way other people did, full of hopeful ideas and plans, and it hurts me that now as an adult others try to label me "once a victim, always a victim" again and again. When that happens I feel like an actor forced to go out on stage every day of her life and give the same monologue. A continuous loop, only in this case the stage is my life and I would like to take on another role for a change.

"I'm trying to get up that great big hill of hope" is part of the song I mentioned above. I don't want to give up hope, because hope is one of the strongest drives that we have. Life is a process where it is less about the outcome then about the journey you travel. My journey is certainly not comparable to one travelled by most people. But no matter how many twists and turns it takes, I simply want to be allowed to take my journey. I would like to shape my life to be as fulfilled as possible and to enjoy my remaining, valuable time with care. I know how important that is, not just as a result of my captivity, but also from the period just after my escape. After all, we only live once, and this is my life.

Appendix

# *Chronology of Events*

*2 March 1998:* On that Monday morning I am thrown into a white delivery vehicle by a man around 7:15 AM on my way to primary school on Brioschiweg. Here, on Melangasse, was where the last day of my old life ended, and when my years of captivity in the hands of my kidnapper, Wolfgang Priklopil, began.

Early that evening my mother filed a "missing persons report" with the Donaustadt district police station. The Vienna Criminal Police Office takes over the case, and the initial search begins in the area surrounding our housing estate at Rennbahnweg, even though the police are still trying to calm fears. Perhaps the girl has simply run away and would turn up the next day, they say. My mother is very certain, "After 48 hours I definitely knew that she would not be disobedient for that long and be sitting in a corner somewhere. Aside from the fact that that is completely unlike her. She is such a reliable girl. She never deviates from her route when walking to school, and she comes straight home again afterwards. Something must've happened."

*3 March 1998:* The first witness speaks up; a 12-year-old girl reports having seen a girl being pulled into a white, tall car (suspected to be a Ford Transit) that then drove away at high speed. She describes two assailants, one at the wheel and the other who pulled me through the sliding door into the vehicle. Her statement will be used repeatedly later on in support of the theory that Priklopil was not acting alone.

*5 March 1998:* The search for me is expanded to all of Austria; up to now it has been limited to the neighbourhood around my school and my mother's flat. One of the investigators tells the press, "We are really groping in the dark here. We have to be open about admitting that."

*15 March 1998:* The Sunday edition of the Austrian daily Kurier reports on an initial lead in the investigation. According to Walter Pöchhacker, a professional detective initially hired by the newspaper who later continued the investigation on his own, police should look for the kidnapper in the girl's immediate environment, saying that there was possibly "someone who knows everything about her disappearance". The hounding of my family begins. The most absurd accusations and suspicions are heaped on my mother more than anyone, and she is downright pilloried in public.

*6 April 1998:* In conjunction with a large-scale search for owners of white delivery vehicles two police officers also pay a visit to Wolfgang Priklopil. He has no police record, is cooperative and willingly shows the officers the vehicle containing construction debris and building materials. There are no witnesses to corroborate his alibi that he was at home on the day and at the time in question. But there is no cause to doubt his statements.

*11 April 1998:* Alleged sex photos of me appear in the Austrian magazine News. My mother had always been more than willing to show visiting journalists pictures of me and our family. Now, some were pocketed while she was in the kitchen making coffee for the journalists in her flat. The snapshots of a girl, who, like all kids, simply liked to dress up, are hyped in the media as pornographic imagery. For some this is evidence that my parents, or their extended circle of family and friends, had either abused me or were planning to sell "indecent" photographs to persons interested in such material.

*14 April 1998:* The investigators receive their first specific tip to look into Wolfgang Priklopil. An anonymous tip from a canine police officer in Vienna. Everything fits: The description of a loner, a suspicion of having a liking for children, possible weapons possession, the address, the house on Heinestraße 60 with its barricaded and secure outward appearance. The tip is filed away.

Later the discussion on errors in the investigation would flare up primarily due to this inadvertent or intended "blunder". The entire issue is greatly inflated by the media. For me, this information, and its subsequent instrumentalization on the political stage, are a bitter pill. At the same time I have tried to develop a certain nonchalance when confronted with revelations like these. It would be misguided to let myself get all worked up, because it wouldn't change the facts one bit. Even if there had been at least one tiny chance of finding me and ending my captivity just six weeks after my disappearance.

*1998 to 2002:* Private investigators and "self-proclaimed" investigators – in other words those without an official mandate – such as family court judge and former National Council member Martin Wabl push the police and the public in every direction. My parents have to submit to a lie detector test; they grasp at straws and allow themselves to be instrumentalized against each other by the media. Divining rod practitioners enter the picture, contact with the afterlife is established, again and again wannabe copycats call claiming to have me in their grasp or to know where my body has been buried.

Unspeakable accusations are heaped primarily on my mother. One claim accuses her of having colluded with a supposed lover to kill me and dump my body in a pond. Another charge was that I had been sexually abused in the family, was planning to go to the police and therefore had to disappear. The most stubborn claim was the suspicion that my mother had something to do with my kidnapping. Retired judge Martin Wabl files a lawsuit against her in 2001 on these grounds. During the trial he is advised by Detective Pöchhacker.

My mother wins the case: in November 2001 the court orders Dr. Wabl to cease and desist from claiming that my mother had anything to do with the kidnapping.

The judgement is upheld on appeal in the last instance. After my escape Wabl demands that the case be reopened, as I am to be considered new "evidence". His petition is granted, and the legal dispute drags on until 2009 – with the same outcome as back in 2001.

*17 July 2002:* The Interior Ministry orders the Vienna Criminal Police Office to relinquish the case to their colleagues in Eisenstadt, the capital of the province of Burgenland, after four years of investigations. A new special task force is set up there, which is to systematically examine the case and review all of the clues. However, it is understaffed and the case file is too extensive.

*23 August 2006:* Around noon I am able to flee after 3,096 days in captivity. The kidnapper is distracted, talking on the phone, and the back garden gate is slightly open. I just take off, sprinting across a narrow gully to Blaselgasse, and from there into an allotment garden. A window is open on one of the houses, and I am able to draw attention to myself. The woman, who calls the police after considerable hesitation, will not, however, allow me into the house asking, "Why did you come to me?" I am panicked and my whole body is trembling for fear that the kidnapper could discover me and drag me back to his house at any second.

That same evening Wolfgang Priklopil jumps in front of a train not far from the Praterstern station in Vienna.

*24 August 2006:* Around one hour after the news of my escape the previous day was sent through the wire and spread through electronic media at high speed, a Canadian man is the first to secure an Internet domain containing the name "Natascha Kampusch". Shortly thereafter all conceivable variations are taken; later my attorneys are to spend days reclaiming these domains in order to prevent their misuse. Some fourteen days later a man attempts to file for protections for the trademark "Natascha Kampusch" at the Patent Office in Munich – fortunately without success.

*25 August 2006:* A DNA report confirms that the "confused young woman" taken into custody in the allotment gardens in Strasshof is in fact "abduction victim Natascha Kampusch". The first press conference is held by the interior minister and the chief investigator.

*28 August 2006:* In my "letter to the world public" I ask the media for calm and restraint until I have regained enough of my strength to provide my own telling of recent events. The letter does not have the hoped-for effect. The race for the first photograph of me enters a new round. Quotes supposedly from me have already been published. Confidential statements I made to police officers and police psychologists are also leaked to the public.

*6 September 2006:* In order to relieve the official pressure and put a lid on continued speculation it is decided that I am to give three interviews: Kronenzeitung, the magazine News and the Austrian Broadcasting Corporation (ORF). The roughly 45-minute television interview is broadcast that evening at 8:15 PM in Austria, and one hour later in Germany. All in all, the broadcast is shown in its entirety in ten European countries, and excerpts from the interview are broadcast in 120 countries.

*21 September 2006:* Criminal proceedings against Wolfgang Priklopil are discontinued due to his death. In November the police also close the file on a man, who – baselessly – was suspected of possibly being involved in my abduction.

*4 October 2006:* German magazine Stern publishes speculations of "S&M rituals with Natascha". Barely six weeks after my escape I am at the focus of increasingly sordid "reporting" that is not even worthy of the name. Where the official events are deemed insufficient, embellishments, distortions and exaggerations are added. To this day this wave has yet to subside. Most often it goes hand-in-hand with suspicions of additional abductors, or even a pornography ring that would have to reach the highest levels – because otherwise it would have long been unearthed. Where there is nothing, there is nothing to reveal. There is nothing more to say on that from my point of view.

*15 November 2006:* The public prosecutor's office confirms that there are no indications that Priklopil had any accomplices. The information does nothing to impede continued speculations concerning additional abductors, as well as alleged "porn videos".

*5 February 2008:* Former head of Austria's Federal Criminal Police Office Haidinger (head of the second special task force in Burgenland) testifies before the Parliamentary Committee on Interior Affairs that there were clues that could have led to the case being solved much earlier on, but had been covered up. The Interior Ministry did not want the issue to become public knowledge, as nobody wanted a police scandal ahead of the general elections.[*]

The Interior Ministry responds by setting up a six-member "evaluation commission" to examine these accusations over the next several months. The head of the commission is retired Constitutional Court

---

[*] http://www.spiegel.de/politik/ausland/fall-kampusch-innenministerium-soll-fahndungspannen-vertuscht-haben-a-533764.html (Version: August 2016)

President Ludwig Adamovich; assisting him is former Supreme Court President Johann Rzeszut, also retired.

*3 March 2008:* A parliamentary fact-finding committee is set up to shed light on the work carried out in various ministries.

*18 April 2008:* The free newspaper Heute publishes fragments from my first interviews with the police. Quotes are taken out of context and shortened beyond recognition. The upshot is that I had voluntarily maintained a sexual relationship with the kidnapper (what could possibly be deemed voluntary under those circumstances?) And possibly given birth to a baby while in captivity. "What happened to the possible baby? Did she lose it, or did it disappear in a manner that has yet to be explained?" wrote the newspaper.

The alleged pregnancy is skilfully brought into connection with the work of the evaluation commission and the fact-finding committee, giving it a veneer of "fact". Subsequently additional details from the police reports, which had been confidential up until then, are made public. They had been provided to the parliamentary committee for the purposes of their investigation. In addition to the confidentiality clause that the members were required to sign.

Several media outlets begin to demand that all of the materials be made available to the public, claiming that everything else would feed suspicions that there had in fact been a cover-up. It is apparently unimportant that the objective was to protect the victim, to uphold her right to privacy. Just the opposite: If I were to take legal action to block such a move, that would only prove that I had a great deal to hide and an interest in never fully clearing up the crime, they write.

*11 June 2008:* The commission's report is submitted to the interior minister. Essentially the report indicates that the "pertinent investigative approaches" had apparently "not been fully implemented" (for example, with regard to the tip provided by the police officer from the canine unit). The report also states that there was no indication of a targeted cover-up.

*23 October 2008:* The press reports that the "Kampusch case" is to be reopened again. One month later the investigative order from the public prosecutor's office reaches the new special task force formed to shed light on the unanswered questions concerning the manner of the original investigations. Franz Kröll is charged with managing the operations of the task force.

Moreover, an additional commission headed up by Adamovich is to help to clear up unanswered questions arising from the evaluation report.

The mandates are actually quite clear. The focus is on facts stemming from the internal handling of my case, not on the continued investigation of the case itself. Nevertheless, the head of the commission specifically redirects the probe, heading into a different, very well-known direction. Once again it is about sex, pornography rings and accomplices. And the accusations of abuse are raised once again. The photographs stolen from my mother could be an indication; perhaps there was even a direct connection between my family and the kidnapper, it is said.

*May 2009 to August 2009:* In the wake of an unpublished interim report from the commission, rumours and speculation are once again stoked. The work of the body set up to examine the processes carried out in various public authorities also leads to my family and myself being discredited once again. In a newspaper interview Adamovich states that my time in captivity was possibly "entirely better" than what I had "experienced before", and that considering the conditions in which I had grown up, assumptions that I was a victim "by coincidence" could not be taken seriously.

My mother files a lawsuit against these claims. In December 2009 Adamovich is found guilty of defamation and ordered to pay a fine of

€ 10,000. His attorney appeals the decision, and one year later the appeal is successful. The appeals court rules that Adamovich's statements were still protected under freedom of opinion.[*]

Even during the hearing before the court of first instance he had claimed that Priklopil had acted on orders and that I was likely covering up for accomplices, because I was being blackmailed with compromising material. In addition, there were "indications" of a "positive, and even loving relationship" between the kidnapper and me. The fact that I was given a cake for my 18th birthday, among other things, did not "dovetail very cleanly with the image of my supposedly lurid captivity," whereas, during the period before my abduction I was in an "unfortunate situation".[**]

I find all of this absurd conjecture extremely humiliating. My time in captivity is made ridiculous, and my behaviour and that of my family is subject to cynical judgment. With their statements, both Adamovich and Rzeszut manage to distract from their actual mandates, transforming me from a victim to a potential accomplice, or at least casting me as liar.

*2 January 2010:* The news magazine Profil writes that I had successfully escaped twice, but returned to Priklopil of my own free will.

*8 January 2010:* Police and public prosecutors hold a press conference where they announce that Wolfgang Priklopil had acted alone. The case is to be closed again, and the special task force formed in October 2008 to be disbanded.

In June 2010 Franz Kröll, the operational head of the task force, is found dead. All indications point to a self-inflicted gunshot wound, which is quickly subject to doubt, giving rise to various theories.

Several months later Johann Rzeszut makes a statement in connec-

---

[*] Der Standard, 23 December 2010
[**] Kronenzeitung, 24 December 2009

tion with the investigator's death, saying that it was necessary to continue investigating. He owed it to Kröll; otherwise he wouldn't be able "to look at himself in the mirror anymore".\* The investigations to date were "considerably and sustainably impeded", and important materials had even been withheld. Kröll had been subject to "unjustifiable pressure", in that he had been "unmistakably" told that the investigation was to be closed. This had happened although "just prior to that there had been an additional, heightened need for clarification in the case". "Only job-related reasons could be considered as the cause of his death."\*\*\*

The competent authorities in Graz characterize the accusations as "completely out of thin air".

*8 September 2010:* My autobiography 3,096 Days is published. In May Constantin Film had announced that Bernd Eichinger wanted to film the story. After his death Sherry Hormann takes over production, and filming is to begin in 2012.

*2 November 2010:* It is announced that the Innsbruck public prosecutor's office is to investigate five public prosecutors from Vienna on suspicion of abuse of office. The basis for the investigation is a so-called memorandum stating the facts of the case sent to Parliament by Johann Rzeszut, claiming that the accused had "consistently and persistently neglected to consider decisive police investigation results".

*3 May 2011:* The Republic of Austria rejects a compensatory payment for my time in captivity, as there had been no grounds for suspecting the kidnapper prior to my escape.

*24 November 2011:* After a ten-month investigation a 600-page report

---

\* Der Standard, 4 November 2010
\*\*http://www.krone.at/Oesterreich/Chefermittler_der_SOKO_Kampusch_in_den_Tod_getrieben-Ex-Richter_klagt_an-Story-225467 (Version: August 2016)

issued by the Innsbruck public prosecutor's office exculpates the five Viennese public prosecutors accused of abuse of office. The case is closed. There is no indication that any steps in the investigation had been knowingly omitted, the report said. In addition, nobody precipitously determined that Priklopil had acted alone; there was simply no indication of any accomplices.

The report offers former Constitutional Court judge Adamovich no cause to change his assessment of his accomplice theory. The far right Austrian Freedom Party (FPÖ) comes to his aid and resurrects – as already mentioned – the story of my supposed "baby". "Strong indications point to this fact," they said, although the medical records issued by the Vienna General Hospital show that a pregnancy had been definitively ruled out. Dr. Friedrich had informed the public prosecutor's office of this back in October 2009, and it was indicated in all of the documents made available to various commissions and committees.

In February 2012 the alleged pregnancy would prompt a police detective, disguised as a lecturer on road safety, to arrive at a school in Laxenburg in order to get a hold of suitable genetic material belonging to a young girl. At least in this scenario, I hadn't murdered the baby, but given it to Ernst H.'s sister to raise. A minor consolation.

Once again, people were becoming involved in the matter, pushed into the public spotlight, who were completely innocent. All of this was due to the fantasies of a number of gentlemen who appeared to have lost any shred of decency, morals or sense of moderation, and primarily any relationship to the facts.

Possible connections between the police detective and former Supreme Court judge Rzeszut are debated in court in early summer 2015. The detective had stated that he was commissioned by Rzeszut, which Rzeszut successfully refuted. However, telephone records for the periods just prior and subsequent to the incident in Laxenburg demonstrate frequent contacts between the two gentlemen. Rzeszut is acquitted of giving false testimony. The court extended to him the benefit of the doubt, determining that the former president of the Supreme Court had simply forgotten to mention his contacts with the detective during his questioning.

*December 2011:* Yet another parliamentary fact-finding committee is formed. As with the first, the committee members are sworn to maintain confidentiality, particularly with regard to the details that could violate my right to privacy.

*May 2012:* Documents from the fact-finding committee are leaked to the media. The leak could not be correctly identified, but it is apparently there. There is talk of a "violation of parliamentary secrecy". Although this constitutes "an enormous breach of trust," says the chairman of the committee, as no documents from a secret committee are to be made public, he was unable to rescind the immunity of the committee members[*]

*June 2012:* It is decided to completely reopen the case once again and to obtain the assistance of outside specialists. Cold case experts from the FBI and Germany's BKA. The press calls the move a "declaration of bankruptcy" on the part of Austria.

*15 April 2013:* These experts as well confirm that it was highly likely that Priklopil acted alone, that he had no connections to ominous pornography rings and that he had in fact killed himself. When asked for a statement on the outcome, I said, "I am happy that international cold case specialists from the FBI and Germany's BKA have determined that there is no evidence for any third-party involvement, in other words no evidence for the theory of accomplices. I hope that this report can put an

---

[*] derstandard.at/1336696770984/Fall-Kampusch-Parlamentarischer-Geheimnisver-rat-bleibt-ohne-Sanktionen (Version: August 2016)

end to the Natascha Kampusch criminal case."

Even today it is incomprehensible to me how many detours were taken, how much time, energy and money were wasted only to arrive at the same exact result. Time and again additional twists and turns were added, such as the suspicion that Priklopil had been laid on the train tracks already dead. Who killed him? Who put him there?

And even if the autopsy report, the statement given by the suburban train engineer and those reports by outside and internal experts stated that there was no justification for doubting his suicide.

*Spring 2016:* This hypothesis is resurrected once again. The brother of the late head of the Vienna Kampusch special task force files a criminal complaint against an unknown person. There was even speculation of murder concerning Franz Kröll's suicide. Johann Rzeszut tells German news magazine Der Spiegel, "The fact that a criminal case with at least one relevant murder suspicion is considered closed, even before all of the key investigative leads have been exhausted, is not something that should go uncontested."*

It is simply one continuous loop without end.

---

* http://www.spiegel.de/panorama/justiz/natascha-kampusch-zweifel-an-suizid-des-entfueh-rers-wolfgang-priklopil-a-1087957.html (Version: August 2016)

# *Acknowledgements*

I would like to thank my family who never forgot me.

I would like to thank all those people who believed in me both during my captivity and after my escape.

I would like to thank all of those who have shown compassion for my situation.

And I would like to thank all of those people who have supported me either personally or professionally and have made so much possible for me.